# Psychological Management
## of Schizophrenia

# Psychological Management of Schizophrenia

*Edited by*

**Max Birchwood**
*All Saints Hospital, Birmingham, UK*

*and*

**Nicholas Tarrier**
*University of Manchester, UK*

JOHN WILEY & SONS
Chichester · New York · Brisbane · Toronto · Singapore

Copyright © 1994 by John Wiley & Sons Ltd,
    Baffins Lane, Chichester,
    West Sussex PO19 1UD, England
    Telephone (+44) 243 779777

Reprinted June 1995

*Other Wiley Editorial Offices*

John Wiley & Sons, Inc., 605 Third Avenue,
New York, NY 10158-0012, USA

Jacaranda Wiley Ltd, 33 Park Road, Milton
Queensland 4064, Australia

John Wiley & Sons (Canada) Ltd, 22 Worcester Road,
Rexdale, Ontario M9W 1L1, Canada

John Wiley & Sons (SEA) Pte Ltd, 37 Jalan Pemimpin #05-04,
Block B, Union Industrial Building, Singapore 2057


*Library of Congress Cataloguing in Publication Data*

Psychological management of schizophrenia / edited by Max Birchwood
    and Nicholas Tarrier.
        p.   cm.
        Selected and updated core chapters of *Innovations in the
    psychological management of schizophrenia.*
        Includes bibliographical references and index.
        ISBN 0-471-95056-4 (pbk.)
        1. Schizophrenia—Treatment.   2. Schizophrenics—Services for.
    I. Birchwood, M. J.   II. Tarrier, Nicholas.   III. Title: Innovations
    in the psychological management of schizophrenia.
    RC514.P71878   1994
    616.89'820651—dc20                                    94–6698
                                                             CIP

*British Library Cataloguing in Publication Data*

A catalogue record for this book is available from the British Library.

ISBN 0-471-95056-4 (paper)


Typeset in 10/12pt Palatino by Mathematical Composition Setters Ltd, Salisbury, Wiltshire
Printed and bound in Great Britain by Biddles Ltd, Guildford and King's Lynn

# Contents

# Contributors

CHRISTINE BARROWCLOUGH    Consultant Clinical Psychologist, Mancunian Community NHS Trust, Baguley Health Centre, Baguley, Manchester, UK

MAX BIRCHWOOD    Consultant Clinical Psychologist, All Saints Hospital, Birmingham, UK and Professor of Psychology and Head of the Academic Unit of Psychology of the Northern Birmingham Mental Health Trust.

VALERIE DRURY    Research Psychologist, Archer Centre, All Saints Hospital, Birmingham, UK.

FRANK HOLLOWAY    Consultant Psychiatrist, Maudsley Hospital, London, UK.

TONY LAVENDER    Joint Director, Clinical Psychology Training Scheme, Salomans Centre, Tunbridge Wells, Kent, UK.

FIONA MACMILLAN    Senior Lecturer in Psychiatry, University of Birmingham and Honorary Consultant Psychiatrist, All Saints Hospital, Birmingham, UK.

JO SMITH    Principal Clinical Psychologist, Barnsley Hall Hospital, Bromsgrove, Hereford and Worcester, UK.

NICHOLAS TARRIER    Professor of Clinical Psychology, University of Manchester, Manchester, UK.

# Preface

This book is published at a time that will be seen in years to come as a watershed in the development of services for people with severe mental disorder. A number of pressures have converged causing a realignment of mental health policy and practice towards this client group.

The closure of our mental hospitals and the pressure on the community to "look after its own" puts a burden not only on families and carers of people with severe mental health problems but also on services to respond to this and to find a means of co-ordinating the fragmentation of services that has resulted. There has been a change too in our models of understanding the psychoses, particularly schizophrenia. The genuine interaction of biological vulnerability and psychological, psychosocial and cultural influences is increasingly understood; the role of the "self" in the appraisal of symptoms and their genesis has also become an exciting area of research. These models have driven a number of innovations in treatment and management that are of proven or promising efficacy. There is also the growing consumer voice of both carer and client, which is beginning to influence the nature, style and delivery of care. Mental health professionals from a variety of disciplines are becoming increasingly sensitive to these pressures, but there is also great excitement at the rapid pace of development and the opportunities created by these new treatment approaches, which together have seen a growing demand for practical skills and new models of care relevant to this disadvantaged and often difficult client group.

This text builds upon the success of our previous volume *Innovations in the Psychological Management of Schizophrenia* and offers a practical guide for mental health professionals wanting to develop and enhance their skills in these new treatment and intervention approaches. We have selected and updated the core chapters, which include: family interventions and network support; early warning systems to anticipate and control relapse; strategies to control distressing symptoms, such as hallucinations and delusions; and improving recovery from acute psychosis. The chapters largely reflect the work in our two centres in Manchester and Birmingham. We have also reviewed in our introductory chapter exciting developments in related areas, including cognitive therapy for hallucinations and delusions, depression and suicide and early intervention in young people with psychosis. We have also included the excellent chapter on Models of Continuing Care by Tony Lavender and Frank Holloway. The latter we feel is particularly important, for without models of implementation, the inertia of systems and vested interests will, we believe, see the coming era of community care as merely a case of "new bottles for old wine".

MAX BIRCHWOOD AND NICHOLAS TARRIER
*January 1994*

Chapter 1

# Making a Reality of the Community Management of Schizophrenia

NICHOLAS TARRIER AND MAX BIRCHWOOD

## INTRODUCTION

The concept of community care or care in the community is no stranger to controversy: lauded as the universal panacea for the seriously and chronically mentally ill and the nemesis of institutional psychiatry, vested interest and poor practice by its more adherent supporters and reviled as woolly and unrealistic, resulting in the harmful and unkind abandonment of those most unable to care for themselves by its detractors. What is the true status of community care? What is achievable and attainable and what is unrealistic?

These are complex and difficult questions and we do not set ourselves up even to attempt to answer them. But what we do maintain is that to be successful, community services for the seriously mentally ill need to be organised coherently and be able to deliver the best available treatments and intervention. This may appear obvious and self-evident but if so why are psychosocial interventions not more readily available? Why are mental health professionals not routinely trained in these methods? Why are mental health services still so strongly linked both in terms of resources and also in terms of staff allegiances to the hospital rather than to a community base?

In this short volume we have put together and revised some of the more practically based chapters from our previously published book *Innovations in the Psychological Management of Schizophrenia: Assessment, Treatment and Services* (Birchwood and Tarrier, 1992) with the aim of making these practical guides to intervention more widely accessible to a larger audience, especially those who are working in the community with patients suffering from a psychotic illness. Our aim is to suggest that psychosocial management methods that could have considerable benefit for psychotic patients are available and can, given the right conditions, be implemented widely.

This, we feel, could be a crucial aspect of the success or failure of community care. The adherence to the philosophy and the will to reorganise services are not sufficient alone and will always be hostage to fortune unless there is a move to innovate and develop therapeutic interventions. We feel that the chapters in our first book described new interventions that are part of a rising tide of innovation in non-drug therapeutic interventions with schizophrenia. These have been carried out mainly in research or pilot service settings and it is important that there is a dissemination and permeation of psychosocial management into the larger arena of community mental health services.

Andrews and Teesson (1994) have argued recently that medical, nursing and mental health staff trained in psychiatric hospitals view schizophrenia, erroneously, as a chronic deteriorating disease, that institutions and their staff will fight to survive and that the attitudes formed in the institutions will abound. As economic considerations bite tighter and harder, the pessimistic view of schizophrenia as being untreatable and largely unmanageable without containment will prevail. Community care will fail under the twin onslaught of "value for money" short-term economics and pessimistic and self-serving staff attitudes. Constant pruning of mental health budgets will, Andrews and Teesson argue, result in mental health services caring for and containing a small population of chronic psychotic patients. They argue further that it does not have to be this way. Treatment methods are available and can be introduced with young early onset psychosis. Furthermore, research has demonstrated that those suffering from mental illness can be served better through home-based treatments than hospital care (Stein and Test, 1980; Hoult, 1986; Muijen, Marks and Connolly, 1992). Too much money is channelled into hospital care and a disproportionately low amount into the community facilities where most mental disorder is managed.

Results from the Team for the Assessment of Psychiatric Services (TAPS) Project (Leff, 1993), in which the policy to evaluate the closure of Claybury and much of Friern Psychiatric Hospitals was carefully evaluated, demonstrated that when carefully planned and financed the closure of a psychiatric hospital does not lead to a marked increase in vagrancy, crime and mortality for the long-term mentally ill (Dayson, 1993). Moreover, patients reintroduced into the community developed more diverse social networks and had a greater opportunity for autonomy than patients in hospital (Anderson et al. 1993). So despite media outcry against deinstitutionalisation, a well-evaluated study of deinstitutionalisation demonstrates that community living for the long-term mentally ill does not mean the abandonment of these patients but can lead to positive benefits if carried out appropriately.

RECENT DEVELOPMENTS

Since our previous volume was published a number of further developments have taken place that confirm our view that psychological management is viable in community care. These developments have largely been
extensions of research tracks that are covered in the chapters here but from
which further results have arisen. We will take this opportunity to outline
some of these results and developments, many of which are as yet
unpublished.

**Family interventions**

A number of well-controlled studies of family intervention (see Chapter 3)
have demonstrated that family interventions can significantly reduce
relapse rates over the first year after discharge. These studies have also
included a 2-year follow-up, which demonstrated that although relapses
increase in the second year, a significant benefit for family intervention is
still maintained. Schizophrenia is a disorder that frequently starts in late
adolescence or early adulthood and continues for the rest of the patient's
life, hence, 2 years as a follow-up period is a very short time. Tarrier and
colleagues (Tarrier et al., in press) have followed up their patient cohort
from the Salford Family Intervention Project through examination of the
psychiatric notes over a longer period, assessing relapse at both 5 years
and at 8 years. Patients were categorised as those who lived with high
Expressed Emotion (EE) families and received family intervention, those
who lived with high EE families and received routine care (high EE control)
and those who lived with low EE families and received routine care (low
EE control). The EE of the relatives was assessed at the initial hospitalisation when the patient and their relatives were recruited into the study. The
family intervention took place over the first 9 months after discharge and
is described in detail in Chapter 3. The relapse results are presented in
Table 1.1 in terms of percentage of patients in the group who relapsed at
each follow-up point: 9 months, 2 years, 5 years and 8 years.

These results indicate that although there is an accumulating increase in
the number of patients who relapse over the extended follow-up period,
a significant difference between the family intervention group and the high
EE control group is maintained for up to 8 years. Despite the fact that over
two-thirds of patients who received family intervention with their families
did eventually relapse, the initial benefits over the control group that were
achieved through family intervention during the first year after discharge
were maintained for up to 8 years. It is also of interest that the differences

Table 1.1  Percentage of patients in the Salford Family Intervention Project who experienced a relapse up to 8 years after discharge

| Group | Relapse rates (%) | | | |
| --- | --- | --- | --- | --- |
|  | 9 months | 2 years | 5 years | 8 years |
| Family intervention | 12 | 33 | 62 | 67 |
| High EE control | 48 | 59 | 83 | 88 |
| Low EE control | 21 | 33 | 65 | 69 |

between high EE and low EE control groups is also evident 5 and 8 years after the initial assessments. Furthermore, there appear strong similarities between the relapse rates in the family intervention group and in the low EE control group.

The Birmingham Family Intervention Project has approached the family management of schizophrenia from a burden or needs perspective, and did not use high EE as an entry point to their intervention. It was established first that the "high EE" classification does not capture all those families in need of intervention in terms of understanding of schizophrenia, subjective and objective burden and perceived coping difficulty. Whereas two-thirds of our high EE group had "high needs" on one or more of these indices, we identified one-third of the low EE group presenting with "high" needs (Smith et al., 1992); this significant subgroup would otherwise be overlooked in an EE-led intervention. The family intervention emphasised the amelioration of family burden and resolution of loss felt by parents in particular. The results (Birchwood et al., in press) show a large and significant reduction in family needs (stress, burden and coping) in the intervention but not in the control group, independent of expressed emotion; and a major improvement in perceived coping efficacy in those receiving intervention, but not the controls, for high EEs only (Figure 1.1). There was a very low level of criticism in the relatives of the young (predominantly first episode) patients studied, and a correspondingly high level of emotional over-involvement (EOI), a result also reported by Stirling et al. (1991, 1993). Intervention had little impact on this low basal rate of criticism (and, therefore, relapses) among the high EE relatives, but did have a major impact on EOI (Figure 1.2). Although the study by Tarrier et al. (1988) found no influence of education alone on relapse, Birchwood, Smith and Cochrane (1992) did find a significant reduction in subjective family burden following group family education. It would seem, therefore, that in the short space of time since our last text, we may be a step nearer to addressing what we regard as a crucial question: "What kind of family intervention is appropriate for what kind of outcome?" (Birchwood, 1992).

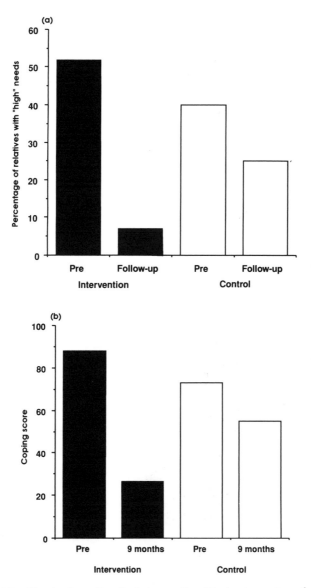

Figure 1.1  The Birmingham Family Intervention Study: impact on family needs.
(a) Changes in percentage of relatives with "high" needs ($P < 0.05$). (b) Changes
in coping scores of high EE relatives only ($P < 0.036$).

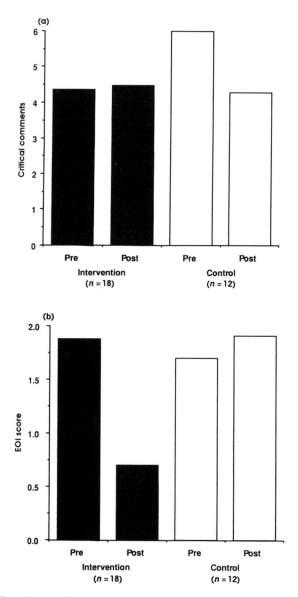

Figure 1.2 The Birmingham Family Intervention Study: impact on expressed emotion, (EE). (a) Changes in critical comments from high EE relatives only (not significant). (b) Changes in emotional over-involvement (EOI) scores of high EE relatives only ($P < 0.03$).

## Dissemination and training

Despite the successful results reported for family interventions, the point has often been made that these results were the product of enthusiastic and highly trained specialist research teams and the case for family interventions working in a normal service setting remains unproven. There is some truth in this argument, although the Salford project was performed by service psychologists attempting to run a district service with a research-funded evaluation team. The potential for family interventions to become standard practice requires two conditions: firstly, the availability of quality training in family intervention methods; and secondly, radical organisational change to accommodate family and psychosocial management as the core management approach for psychosis.

Some progress has been achieved in training. The Department of Nursing at Manchester University set up a project in 1988 to train community psychiatric nurses (CPNs) in family management methods and to evaluate the effectiveness of this training. This project was stimulated by the research results reporting the benefits of family intervention and also by concern over the "drift" in the role and activity of CPNs. Community psychiatric nurse services had been established in the mid-1950s for the after-care and follow-up of psychotic patients receiving the newly introduced neuroleptics (Simmons and Brooker, 1986). Recent evidence suggested that CPNs were spending considerably less time with psychotic patients than non-psychotic affective disordered patients (Wooff, Goldberg and Fryers, 1988) and that schizophrenic patients "constituted a mere 27% of all total CPN caseloads throughout the UK" (White, 1990). The advances in therapeutic interventions appear not to have been reflected in CPN training and the lack of skills in psychosocial interventions had resulted in CPNs "drifting" away from contact with patients with psychoses. So a training scheme was devised, which aimed to train CPNs in family intervention and provide them with clinical supervision with the hope that the provision of these skills and clinical supervision would rekindle interest in working with psychotic patients.

In the initial trial (Brooker et al., 1992) nine CPNs were recruited from three regional Health Authorities through advertisement. Each selected CPN was matched with a colleague from the same health authority on a number of variables, such as length of experience as a CPN, amount of post-qualification training, age and sex. The aim of the study was for each CPN to recruit three schizophrenic patients and their families into their caseload, a total of 54 families. Initially 87% of the target was achieved; however, 17 of these families dropped out during the 1-year follow-up. The 30 families who completed the trial represented 64% of the recruited sample. All CPNs, both experimental and control, were trained in the

clinical assessment methods and the nine experimental CPNs attended a
training course in family management derived from that used in the
Salford project (see Barrowclough and Tarrier, 1992). The course was of 6
months duration and consisted of didactic and workshop teaching, and
clinical supervision throughout the 6 months. The continuous clinical
supervision was considered an essential constituent of the course and was
led by clinical psychologists experienced in the area. Evaluation of the
patients and families indicated that there were small but significant
improvements in patients' symptomatology. Depression, anxiety, delusions and physical retardation improved in patients managed by the CPNs
who were receiving training, whereas only delusions improved in the control group. There was a trend towards a reduction in neuroleptic medication for patients in the experimental group that was not evident in the
control group. Furthermore, there was evidence for significant improvements in personal functioning and social functioning in the experimental
group but not the control group. There was also evidence that relatives of
patients in the experimental group showed a significant decrease in the
presence of minor psychological symptoms as measured by the GHQ
while there was no change in the control group. Such differences may indicate a decrease in the perceived or subjective burden of care in relatives
who received family intervention compared to those who did not. Interestingly, this result contrasts to that of Tarrier and colleagues who report no
changes in GHQ scores for relatives who participated in family intervention (Tarrier et al., 1988). An evaluation of knowledge about schizophrenia
held by the relatives using the KASI evaluation method (Barrowclough et
al., 1987) found that relatives in the experimental group significantly
increased their functional knowledge about schizophrenia whereas the
control group did not (Brooker, Barrowclough and Tarrier, 1992).

  In a subsequent study Brooker and colleagues (Brooker et al., in press)
carried out a within-subject design trial of CPN training in which ten CPNs
recruited six patients and their families, of which three patients and families received family intervention and the other three acted as controls.
After the 6-month follow-up data were collected, the control families were
then offered active family intervention and 65% of the group accepted.
Seventy-eight per cent of families in the intervention group and 96% of
control families remained in the study until follow-up. The family intervention in this study was taught by Falloon and his colleagues (see Falloon,
Boyd and McGill, 1984). The patients who received the intervention
showed a significant improvement in positive and negative symptoms
and a significant increase in social functioning. There was also evidence for
a dramatic decline in hospital usage when mean hospital days per
patient were compared between the 12 months prior to the intervention
and a comparable period after intervention. The experimental group

demonstrated a decline from 18.4 days per annum before treatment to 1.8 days per annum after treatment. In the untreated controls this figure increases from a baseline of 23.5 days per annum to 73.5 days.

Both studies carried out by Brooker and his colleagues in Manchester indicate the positive benefits of training CPNs in family intervention, even though two different types of intervention were used by different groups of workers.

In an Australian study of family intervention training, Kavanagh and his colleagues (Kavanagh et al., 1993) trained mental health workers in a cognitive-behavioural approach to family intervention. However, despite the considerable efforts by the research team, their training appeared to have little impact upon clinical practice, with few of the trainees actually engaging families for any length of time. Trainees received 30–35 hours of didactic and workshop training and then were asked to participate in a controlled evaluation of family intervention by acting as trial therapists. Initially 160 therapists received training but only 44 of these elected to take part in the treatment trial and 28 of these saw only one family. In fact, 57% of the families in the study were seen by six therapists. Therapists reported particular difficulty in integrating the family work with their other duties and interests. Only 4% of the sample reported that their knowledge of cognitive-behavioural approaches was a significant problem but in a written test most therapists failed to demonstrate even the minimum recall of the material they had been taught (Kavanagh et al., 1993). The authors report that in families receiving intervention, 13% of patients receiving family intervention had experienced a marked exacerbation of symptoms compared to 27% in the group who received an individual intervention (Kavanagh et al., 1993). But they conclude "as a demonstration that the structured family intervention could be disseminated into routine community health practice, the project clearly was of limited success".

There are two possible reasons why the training programme of Kavanagh and colleagues yielded such poor results compared to the comparative success of Brooker and colleagues. Successful training requires continuity and progressive clinical supervision, and time-limited didactic and workshop teaching is unlikely to result in skill acquisition in the absence of guided practice. Without supervision within a structured teaching programme, trainees will abandon the new approach very quickly. The second important factor is the necessity for management commitment to the training and practice of the new approach. In Kavanagh's programme there appears to have been little in the way of management commitment to the reorganisation of workloads so that family intervention could be given a high priority. It appears that for most trained therapists in this study, family work was just one more activity that had to be completed in an already overloaded schedule; it is perhaps not surprising that very few therapists attempted to implement what they had been taught without management prioritising of their family work and clinical supervision to shape their practice.

An ongoing project funded by The Jules Thorn Charitable Trust is dedicated to evaluating the training of CPNs in problem-oriented case management, which will include training in three modules: family intervention; psychological management of psychotic symptoms; and case management. The Thorn Nurse Project is taking place in Manchester and London and is supervised in the former by Professors Butterworth and Tarrier and Ms Gill Haddock and in the latter by Professors Craig, Leff and Marks, Ms C. Gambrill and colleagues. The training effectiveness is being evaluated extensively, with the assessment of knowledge and skills acquired by the nurses being assessed by academic measures and evidence of practical skills assessed through clinical casework. Trainees will also assess the clinical effectiveness of their work through the use of standardised clinical assessments and monitoring of problems and goals. An objective clinical assessment will be performed by an independent evaluator on a sample of the patients and their relatives.

The ultimate aim of the project is to "seed" trained nurses into mental health services where they will influence others to create a culture-oriented and problem-oriented case management involving psychosocial management. Eventually satellite training centres may be set up to increase access of various professionals to training in these methods.

## The psychological management of positive psychotic symptoms

### Coping skill enhancement

Since the writing of Chapter 5 on the management of positive symptoms, specifically hallucinations and delusions, the controlled trial of two cognitive-behavioural treatments, Coping Strategy Enhancement (CSE) and Problem Solving (PS), outlined in the chapter has been completed. Twenty-seven patients finally entered the trial and completed post-treatment assessment and 23 completed the 6-month follow-up assessment (Tarrier et al., 1993a). Patients who received cognitive-behaviour therapy demonstrated a significant decrease in their positive psychotic symptoms whereas there was no change in symptoms during the waiting time control period. There was some evidence to indicate that CSE was superior to PS in reducing symptoms, especially in the reduction of delusions. Figure 1.3 indicates the reduction of delusions as measured by the Psychiatric Assessment Scale (Krawiecka et al., 1977), showing a significantly greater decrease in patients who received CSE.

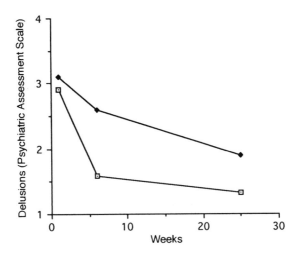

Figure 1.3   Changes in delusions (measured on the Psychiatric Assessment Scale) suffered by patients undergoing treatment with Coping Strategy Enhancement (□) and Problem Solving (◆).

Both groups also demonstrated changes that we regarded as being clinically significant as well as statistically significant. Figure 1.4 shows the percentage of patients in both groups who demonstrated a decrease of 50% or more in their psychotic symptoms. These changes are impressive because on recruitment into the study patients were not showing further symptom reduction despite optimum neuroleptic medication.

Coping and problem-solving skills were also assessed (Tarrier et al., 1993b) and it was found that patients who received CSE significantly improved their coping skills and that improvements in coping were significantly related to decreases in hallucinations and delusions, whereas patients who received PS did not show an improvement in coping skills. All patients showed an improvement in problem-solving skills, whether they received CSE or PS, and improvements in problem-solving skills were not related to symptomatic improvement.

These results were considered promising because of the dramatic improvements that some patients showed over a relatively short period of time with a small number of sessions. Each intervention consisted of 10 sessions spread over 5 weeks. We have now embarked on another study, funded by the Wellcome Trust (Tarrier, Yusupoff and Kinney, 1993), which combines both CSE and PS with a further intervention designed to teach the patient to identify early signs of relapse and to use their coping skills to abort the relapse. It is reasoned that a much longer intervention, which will consist of 30 sessions over 3 months and combines coping skills,

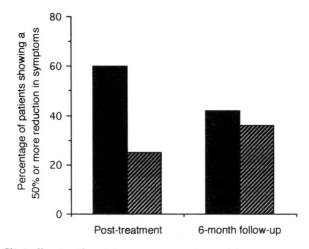

Figure 1.4   Clinically significant improvements in positive symptoms after treatment with Coping Strategy Enhancement (■) and Problem Solving (▨).

problem-solving skills and relapse prevention skills, will have a greater impact on the patient by reducing symptomatology and increasing functioning than did the short intervention of the first trial. It is also anticipated that non-specific factors will be important, especially the building of a strong therapeutic relationship, but to control for the effect of non-specific factors alone a supportive counselling control intervention of the same duration is included, as is a non-treatment control group. We will also examine factors that predict treatment response; in a retrospective analysis of the data from the first trial we found affective flattening and alogia, but not avolition, anhedonia or attention on the Scale for Assessment of Negative Symptoms (SANS) to be related to outcome. Affective flattening here is defined as a "characteristic impoverishment of emotional expression, reactivity and feeling", while alogia refers to an "impoverished thinking and cognition". Hence, patients who show negative symptoms characterised by a poverty of emotion and thought appear not to respond well to cognitive-behavioural approaches. This may be an important finding if replicated patients who are likely to respond well to psychological treatment approaches can be identified and prioritised. We intend to investigate this further and in more detail.

*Cognitive approaches to hallucinations and delusions*

Whilst there is a long tradition within psychology of studying how beliefs are formed and maintained, only recently has this methodological and theoretical expertise been applied to delusions. However, although off to a late start, the psychological study of delusions has called into question traditional psychiatric definitions, elucidated specific examples of cognitive bias and the formation and maintenance of delusions, and uncovered the possible motivational nature of paranoid thinking (Chadwick and Birchwood, 1995). Traditional definitions of delusion have included being held with total and unshakeable convictions, being impervious to other experiences and being of bizarre or of impossible content. In other words, delusions were defined on the basis of discontinuity with normal beliefs. However, Garety and her colleagues have applied sophisticated psychological measures to monitor a number of different dimensions of delusional thinking and have shown that in fact conviction is not always total or unchanging, and that there are times when delusions are sensitive to other experiences (see Garety, 1991). Whilst these studies support the idea that people usually seek only to confirm their delusions, psychological research has established that their confirmation bias is present with all strongly held beliefs, both delusional and non-delusional.

This new emphasis on continuity, as well as discontinuity and delusional thinking, obliges researchers and clinicians to be precise when discussing cognitive processes in delusion formation and maintenance. Garety (1991) reviews the empirical status of five models of delusion formation—abnormalities in personality (e.g. unresolved conflicts), brain state, affect, perception and judgment—and concludes that there is probably no one single pathway to all delusions. There is evidence that some delusions are reasonable interpretations of a perceptual abnormality and that others reflect abnormal reasoning (e.g. "jumping to conclusions"). Garety integrates this evidence with knowledge of normal belief formation to construct a model that specifies precisely the points of departure from normality and illustrates how abnormal perception and judgment may lie at opposite ends of one dimension of delusion formation.

There is strong evidence from research into numerous disorders (e.g. depression, eating disorders and paranoia) that information processing is content specific, i.e. how information is processed depends on its degree of personal significance. Being contextual, this "top down" characteristic is a case of bias rather than deficit. Bentall (1992) describes several types of cognitive bias, implicit in the maintenance of paranoid delusions. These include selective attention to threat, and a characteristic attributional style of making external attributions for negative events and internal attributions for valued outcomes. Bentall's research and attributional bias in paranoia emphasises the social nature of many delusions and is beginning to shed light on the possible motivational nature of these beliefs. It is remarkable that the paranoid's attributional style is in sharp contrast to that implicated in the maintenance of depressive thinking—namely, a tendency to make internal attributions for negative events. The possibility that paranoia is a form of camouflage depression (Zigler and Glick, 1988) is consistent with the attributional research and has received empirical support from a recent study by Bentall (1992). In the case of auditory hallucinations, however, those who believe their voices are punishing or persecuting ("malevolent") are four times *more* likely to be depressed than those who do not (Chadwick and Birchwood, in press), which suggests that if a form of defence exists, it is counterproductive.

There have also been developments in the cognitive approach to auditory hallucinations. Psychological treatment approaches have tended to concentrate on reducing or eliminating either the hallucinatory experience itself or the consequent distress (presumably because distress was seen as an inevitable consequence of hearing voices). However, in a recent study conducted in Birmingham, it was found that the distress occasioned by voices is linked not simply to the fact or content of hallucinations but to the *beliefs* that patients continue to hold about them (Chadwick and Birchwood, 1994). All voices were appraised by patients as being extremely powerful ("omnipotent") but additional beliefs about the voices' identity and purpose meant that some were interpreted as benevolent and others malevolent—this latter distinction has a striking impact on people's behavioural and effective response to voices. All people who believe their voices to be malevolent were distressed when the voices spoke and resisted them by shouting back, seeking distraction and avoiding cues that actuated the voices; all those who believe their voices to be "benevolent" courted them and found them predominantly reassuring, amusing, etc. Furthermore, how voices were interpreted did not follow obviously from the content, as anticipated by the cognitive model. For example, one woman's voice identified itself as coming from God, yet she disregarded this and believed the voice to be from the devil. Conversely, many voices were construed as benevolent, even though they urged suicide and murder.

These cognitive formulations of hallucinations and delusions provide a new target and approach for treatment. Beck, Rush and Shaw (1979) have shown how particular negative beliefs (e.g. "I am worthless") are implicated in the maintenance of depression and that systematically disputing and testing these beliefs in cognitive therapy constitutes an effective treatment; so too, weakening beliefs about voices might greater reduce associated distress and problem behaviour. Cognitive therapy has been adapted for work with voices and preliminary results are encouraging (Chadwick and Birchwood, 1994; 1995). Changes in people's beliefs about their voices' omnipotence, identity and purpose have been associated with reduced distress, problem behaviour and objective burden. Also, early results suggest that weakening beliefs about voices may lead to a reduction in both "malevolent" and "benevolent" voice activity: this possibility is currently being investigated on a large-scale study to assess the usefulness of cognitive therapy for voices.

With regard to delusions, the approach of Chadwick and Lowe (1990) has heralded a significant breakthrough in the cognitive management of delusions. Their interventions involved a highly structured approach to cognitive therapy, eliciting and reviewing the "evidence" for each belief within an atmosphere of "collaborative empiricism". They report a number of well-controlled single case experiments conducted weekly over 20 weeks, showing major reductions in belief conviction.

## Depression and suicide

Community care and the normalisation ethos that frequently accompanies it, places expectations on the individual to achieve socially valued goals, such as marriage, work and so on. For many people with schizophrenia, these are not always achievable and recently there have been a spate of well-publicised cases of suicide. Suicide, which may affect up to 10% of this group, is associated with a history of depression and risk for psychotic relapse (Johnson, 1988). There have been few attempts to address this problem from a psychological point of view, which is surprising in view of the well-established benefits of cognitive therapy for depression (Dobson, 1989). One reason for this apparent neglect may lie in the psychiatric doctrine that depression is a subordinate syndrome to the positive symptoms. Indeed, there is considerable empirical support for this relationship because dysphoria precedes (Birchwood, Smith and Macmillan, 1989), coexists with (Leff, Tress and Edwards, 1988) and is followed by (McGlashan and Carpenter, 1976) depressive symptoms. However, depression surrounding acute episodes may be different from a depression that emerges as a chronic or occurring feature because it can, and often does, present without ongoing positive symptoms (Johnson, 1981). It is also established that depression occurs independently of negative symptoms and drug side-effects (Delisi, 1990).

The results of a recent study have shown that cognitive factors are at play in the phenomenology of depression in schizophrenia (Birchwood et al., 1993). Studying patients who were at least 6 months beyond their acute episode, it was found that the prevalence of depression was high (29%) and closely linked to two cognitive themes. The first was *powerlessness*, in which the individual believed that they had lost control over their mental functioning and that relapse and mental disintegration was uncontrollable and inevitable. Second, a set of *negative self-evaluations* were also identified: firstly, that as the individual is responsible for his symptoms and, hence, blameworthy; second, that as the individual cannot reach his or her aspirations (e.g. marriage, education), then he or she is *ipso facto* unworthy. These were gender-linked and underscored gender differences in depression. We have identified recently a third set of cognitions that underpin depression. We have found (Chadwick and Birchwood, in press) that those who attribute malevolence to their voices are four times more likely to be depressed (80%) than those who construe them as "benevolent". A detailed prospective study is now under way, funded by The Mental Health Foundation, to tease out these varying cognitive foundations of depression in schizophrenia and to inform a trial of cognitive therapy that is presently in preparation.

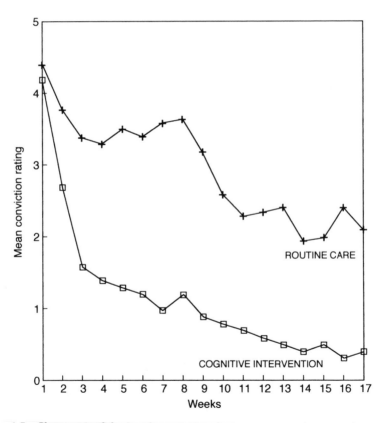

Figure 1.5   Changes in delusional conviction during recovery: intervention versus control (*n* = 19).

### Cognitive intervention in recovery from acute psychosis

Since the publication of the first book, Drury and Birchwood (1994) have now completed an intervention study evaluating a form of cognitive therapy and stress limiting intervention to promote recovery and improve outcomes in acute psychosis. In essence, they find that when comparing full intervention with two control groups, 65% of the intervention group achieved full symptomatic recovery by 12 weeks, compared to 40% of the controls. The difference in patients' rating of conviction in their core delusional beliefs showed early divergence between experimental and control groups (see Figure 1.5). Traditional models of acute care are rather limited to medication and diversion; although there have been attempts to deliver acute treatment under varying degrees of asylum, for example using home treatment strategies (Muijen, Marks and Connolly, 1992), these change the *setting* for traditional medical care rather than the care itself. These early results of cognitive therapy are impressive and have the potential to put "flesh on the bones" of home treatment and change the nature of institutionally focused acute care.

### Early intervention

A research study is in progress evaluating the efficacy of early intervention. The main finding has been that in the large sample of patients studied who were at high risk of psychotic relapse, the rate of relapse and readmission has fallen dramatically and is reflected in indices such as hospital days and use of compulsory admission (Table 1.2). The main manipulation is a pharmacological one (active versus placebo) and the study at the time of writing is still ongoing in order to accumulate sufficient numbers of patients to have sufficient statistical power for this comparison. Birchwood (1994) also outlines the theoretical basis for a form of *cognitive* early intervention, which

Table 1.2  Analysis of admissions and days in admission 2 years pre- and post-trial entry[*]

|  | Pre-trial entry | Post-trial entry |
| --- | --- | --- |
| No. (%) of patients admitted | 26 (74%) | 9 (26%) |
| Total no. of admissions for group | 31 | 10 |
| No. of compulsory admissions | 13 | 1 |
| Days in hospital | 2781 | 729 |

[*] Those patients entering the trial after a first admission are excluded; $n = 35$.

centres on the attributions that clients make about their earliest symptoms of relapse and outlines cognitive strategies for relapse prevention.

There is a second approach that also goes by the name of "Early Intervention" that has been characterised recently (Birchwood and Macmillan, 1993) which is more an approach to care than treatment *per se*. Traditionally, the management of schizophrenia is characterised by two paradigms. The first approaches schizophrenia as episodic relapsing disorders, where treatment is provided through both acute (crisis) care and prophylaxis. The second paradigm, sometimes arising from the failure of the first, is of "rehabilitation" involving amelioration of disabilities, occasionally within a framework of relative asylum. A third paradigm, "Early Intervention" has been proposed involving a combination of medical and psychosocial interventions targeted at young, vulnerable people with the aim of preventing or limiting likely social, psychological and mental deterioration. Evidence is presented showing that the first 5 years are a "critical period" and that vigorous intervention early in the course of illness, early recognition and treatment of relapse and the promotion of psychological adjustment to psychotic illness should be key elements of this third paradigm. In Birmingham, this new "paradigm of care" is being evaluated to see whether vigorous early intervention of this sort is of benefit in preventing symptoms and disability and has an impact disproportionate to, for example, a similar intervention conducted with individuals having longer, more established disorders.

### Community rehabilitation

Another ongoing project in Manchester is aimed at combining some of these new psychological interventions with more traditional self-care and survival skill rehabilitation programmes into a general package that will be delivered to the patients in their own homes (Tarrier et al., 1993c). We are attempting to combine some of the knowledge gained from our research into psychosocial management into a practical community-focused rehabilitation service. This home-based rehabilitation scheme is being carried out in South Manchester and is being evaluated against the traditional hospital-based rehabilitation scheme. We are anticipating that the results of this project will inform us on the practicalities of transporting research results into a community-based district service.

## CONCLUSION

Despite the doubts that have been expressed about the principles and practice of caring for the long-term mentally ill in the community, there is good evidence to suggest that this can be done well when properly planned and appropriately financed. We have also suggested that new and innovative psychological and psychosocial management methods have much to offer such community care. We are both involved with ongoing research in this area and we have expanded further on this in this introductory chapter. Our aim is that more clinicians and mental health service professionals will take up the challenge to provide quality services utilising these methods and the chapters contained in this slim volume will be of assistance to them both to provide community care and also to stimulate further research into this important area.

## REFERENCES

Anderson, J., Dayson, D., Wills, W., Gooch, C., Margolius, O., O'Driscoll, C. and Leff, J. (1993) The TAPS Project. 13: Clinical and social outcomes of long-stay psychiatric patients after one year in the community. *British Journal of Psychiatry*, **162** (suppl. 19), 45–56.

Andrews, G. and Teesson, M. (1994) Smart treatment versus dumb treatment: services for mental disorders. *Current Opinion in Psychiatry*, **6**, 181–185.

Barrowclough, C. and Tarrier, N. (1992) *Families of Schizophrenic Patients: Cognitive Behavioural Intervention*, Chapman & Hall, London.

Barrowclough, C., Tarrier, N., Watts, S., Vaughn, C., Bamrah, J.S. and Freeman, H.L. (1987) Assessing the functional knowledge about schizophrenia: a preliminary report. *British Journal of Psychiatry*, **151**, 1–8.

Beck, A.T., Rush, A.J. and Shaw, B.F. (1979) *Cognitive Therapy of Depression*. New York: Guilford.

Bentall, R. (1992) Reconstructing psychopathology, *The Psychologist*, **5**, 61–6.

Birchwood, M. (1992) Family factors in psychiatry. *Current Opinion in Psychiatry*, **5**, 295–9.

Birchwood, M. (1994) Cognitive early intervention. In: Haddock, G. and Slade, P. (eds), *Cognitive Behavioural Approaches to Schizophrenia*, Routledge, London.

Birchwood, M. and Tarrier, N. (1992) *Innovations in the Psychological Management of Schizophrenia: Assessment, Treatment and Services*, John Wiley, Chichester.

Birchwood, M. and Macmillan, J. (1993) Early intervention in schizophrenia. *Australian and New Zealand Journal of Psychiatry*, **27**, 374–77.

Birchwood, M., Smith, J. and Macmillan, J. (1989) Predicting relapse in schizophrenia: an early signs monitoring system. *Psychological Medicine*, **19**, 649–56.

Birchwood, M., Smith, J. and Cochrane, R. (1992) Specific and non-specific effects of educational intervention for families living with schizophrenia: a comparison of three methods. *British Journal of Psychiatry*, **161**, 783–90.

Birchwood, M., Mason, R., Macmillan, F. and Healy, J. (1993) Depression demoralisation and control over psychotic illness. *Psychological Medicine*, **23**, 387–95.

Birchwood, M., Smith, J., Cochrane, R. and George, S. (in press) A trial of a needs led family intervention in schizophrenia emphasising burden and loss.

Brooker, C., Barrowclough, C. and Tarrier, N. (1992) Evaluating the impact of training community psychiatric nurses to educate relatives about schizophrenia. *Journal of Clinical Nursing*, **1**, 19–25.

Brooker, C., Tarrier, N., Barrowclough, C., Butterworth, A. and Goldberg, D. (1992) Training community psychiatric nurses for psychosocial intervention: report of a pilot study. *British Journal of Psychiatry*, **160**, 836–44.

Brooker, C., Falloon, I.R.H., Butterworth, A., Goldberg, D., Graham-Hole, V. and Hillier, V. (in press) The outcome of training community psychiatric nurses to deliver psychosocial intervention, (in press).

Chadwick, P. and Birchwood, M. (1994) Challenging the omnipotence of voices: a cognitive approach to auditory hallucinations. *British Journal of Psychiatry*.

Chadwick, P. and Birchwood, M. (1995) *Cognitive Therapy for Hallucinations and Delusions*, Wiley, Chichester.

Chadwick, P. and Birchwood, M. (in press) The omnipotence of voices: malevolent beliefs are strongly associated with depression.

Chadwick, P. and Lowe, C. (1990) Measurement and modification of delusional beliefs. *Journal of Consulting and Clinical Psychology*, **58**, 225–32.

Dayson, D. (1993) The TAPS Project. 12: Crime, vagrancy, death and readmission of the long-term mentally ill during their first year of local reprovision. *British Journal of Psychiatry*, **162** (suppl. 19), 40–4.

Delisi, L.E. (ed.) (1990) *Depression in Schizophrenia*, Washington, DC: American Psychiatric Press.

Dobson, K.S. (1989) A meta analysis of cognitive therapy for depression. *Journal of Consulting and Clinical Psychology*, **57**, 414–19.

Drury, V. and Birchwood, M. (1994) Cognitive therapy in acute psychosis: a controlled trial. In preparation.

Falloon, I.R.H., Boyd, J.L. and McGill, C.W. (1984) *Family Care of Schizophrenia*, Guilford Press, New York.

Garety, P. (1991) Reasoning and delusions. *British Journal of Psychiatry*, **159**, (suppl. 14), 14–19.

Hoult, J. (1986) Community care of the acutely mentally ill. *British Journal of Psychiatry*, **149**, 137–44.

Johnson, D.A.W. (1981) Studies of depressive symptoms in schizophrenia. *British Journal of Psychiatry*, **139**, 89–101.

Johnson, D.A.W. (1988) The significance of depression in the prediction of relapse in chronic schizophrenia. *British Journal of Psychiatry*, **152**, 320–3.

Kavanagh, D., Clark, D., Piatkowska, O., O'Halloran, P., Manicavasagar, V., Rosen, A. and Tennant, C. (1993) Application of cognitive-behavioural family intervention for schizophrenia in multidisciplinary teams: what can the matter be? *Australian Psychologist*, **28**, 1–8.

Krawiecka, M., Goldberg, D. and Vaughn, M. (1977) Standardised psychiatric assessment scale for chronic psychiatric patients. *Acta Psychiatrica Scandinavica*, **36**, 25–31.

Leff, J. (ed.) (1993) The TAPS Project: evaluating community placement of long-stay psychiatric patients. *British Journal of Psychiatry*, **162**, (suppl. 19), 4–56.

Leff, J., Tress, K. and Edwards, B. (1988) The clinical course of depressive symptoms in schizophrenia. *Schizophrenia Research*, **1**, 25–30.

McGlashan, T.H. and Carpenter, W.T. (1976) An investigation of the postpsychotic depressive syndrome. *American Journal of Psychiatry*, **133**, 14–19.

Muijen, M., Marks, I. and Connolly, J. (1992) Home-based care and standard hospital care for patients with severe mental illness. *British Medical Journal*, **304**, 749–54.

Simmons, S. and Brooker, C. (1986) *Community Psychiatric Nursing: a Social Perspective*, Heinemann, London.

Smith, J., Birchwood, M., Cochrane, R. and George, S. (1992) The needs of high and low expressed emotion families: normative approach. *Social Psychiatry and Psychiatric Epidemiology*, **28**, 11–16.

Stein, L.I. and Test, M.A. (1980) Alternatives to mental hospital treatment. I: Conceptual model, treatment program and clinical evaluation. *Archives of General Psychiatry*, **137**, 392–7.

Stirling, J., Tantam, D., Thomas, P., Newby, D., Montague, N. and Ring, N. (1991) Expressed emotion and early onset schizophrenia: a one year follow-up. *Psychological Medicine*, **21**, 675–85.

Stirling, J., Tantam, D., Thomas, P., Newby, D., Montague, N. and Rang, N. (1993) Expressed emotion and schizophrenia. The ontogeny of EE during an 18 month follow-up. *Psychological Medicine*, **23**, 771–8.

Tarrier, N., Yusupoff, L. and Kinney, C. (1993) A psychological intervention programme to reduce positive symptoms and prevent relapse in psychotic patients, Project grant, London: The Wellcome Trust.

Tarrier, N., Barrowclough, C., Porceddu, K. and Watts, S. (1988) Distress in the relatives of schizophrenic patients as measured by the GHQ: the effect of family intervention, (unpublished data).

Tarrier, N., Beckett, R., Harwood, S., Baker, A., Yusupoff, L. and Ugarteburu, I. (1993a) A trial of two cognitive-behavioural methods of treating drug-resistant psychotic symptoms in schizophrenic patients: I. Outcome. *British Journal of Psychiatry*, **162**, 524–32.

Tarrier, N., Sharpe, L., Beckett, R., Harwood, S., Baker, A. and Yusupoff, L.(1993b) A trial of two cognitive-behavioural methods of treating drug-resistant psychotic symptoms in schizophrenic patients: II. Treatment specific changes in coping and problem solving skills. *Social Psychiatry and Psychiatric Epidemiology*, **28**, 5–10.

Tarrier, N., Sellwood, W., Jones, S., Thomas, C., Clowes, J. and Hilton, J. (1993c) Home-based rehabilitation programme to patients discharged from hospital with schizophrenia, Manchester, UK: North West Region Health Authority Medical Innovation Fund Project.

Tarrier, N., Barrowclough, C., Porceddu, K. and Fitzpatrick, E. (in press) The Salford Family Intervention Project for schizophrenic relapse prevention: five and eight year accumulating relapses. *British Journal of Psychiatry*.

White, E. (1990) *The Third National Quinquennial Survey of Community Psychiatric Services*, CPNA Publications, Leeds.

Wooff, K., Goldberg, D. and Fryers, T. (1988) The practice of community psychiatric nursing and mental health social work in Salford. *British Journal of Psychiatry*, **152**, 783–92.

Zigler, E. and Glick, M. (1988) Is paranoid schizophrenia really a camouflaged depression? *American Psychologist*, **43**, 284–90.

# Chapter 2

# Recovery from Acute Psychosis

VALERIE DRURY

## INTRODUCTION

Monitoring schizophrenic patients *in remission* in order to detect early signs of relapse may prove a very worthwhile exercise if a florid episode can be forestalled or prevented by early mobilisation of medical and other interventions (see Chapter 4). Monitoring a patient's *recovery* from an acute episode of schizophrenia by mapping the changes in mental state and non-psychotic symptoms (e.g. anxiety, dysphoria), together with gains in insight and disintegration of delusional beliefs may on the face of it look little more than an academic exercise. However, in reality the implications of such an exercise can be many fold. The monitoring process may facilitate the building of rapport between patient and professional with the consequence that the relationship itself may become therapeutic and thus acts as a "safe" environment in which psychological interventions can be introduced and where the patient knows his or her symptoms will be taken seriously. Monitoring could provide the means for measuring efforts to accelerate recovery through psychological intervention and inform the timing and intensity of rehabilitative efforts. Furthermore, monitoring may have medical implications as close observation of non-psychotic symptoms may provide the clinician with supplementary information about the ideal time for medication reduction and discharge.

Detailed, careful monitoring as part of a continuing dialogue between the professional, patient and carers can help to build a "collaborative ethos" in which patient and families regard themselves as partners in the management of schizophrenia (Smith and Birchwood, 1990). Thus participating in a monitoring exercise may be of benefit for patients in its own right in that patients feel they have more "control" over the progression of their illness.

In this chapter there will be an emphasis on practical strategies used to monitor recovery and a demonstration, by the use of case examples, how the information obtained can be of real clinical benefit.

The literature contains little detailed information on duration of recovery and its relationship with variables such as sex, diagnosis and ethnicity. In a retrospective study by Birchwood et al. (in press) of 169 patients admitted for the first time to psychiatric care with an acute psychotic illness, Asians were found to have a significantly briefer period of in-patient care (7.2 weeks) than whites (9.8 weeks), who in turn had a briefer period of in-patient care than Caribbeans (12.8 weeks). In a prospective study by the Early Signs Research Group (in preparation) of 30 in-patients with a clinical diagnosis of schizophrenia, the mean duration of admission was 17.0 weeks: 19.0 weeks for males and 12.3 weeks for females. Availability of suitable accommodation and good family support networks appeared to be important factors in the earlier discharge of the female patients. Thus length of hospitalisation may be an insensitive instrument for measuring the time taken to recover from an acute psychotic episode. In this chapter I shall review the evidence which suggests that recovery cannot be conceptualised as a smooth, linear progression. Individuals appear to pass through qualitatively different phases, sometimes passing back and forth following a "stormy course" in which "psychological", "psychosocial" and "illness" processes interact—an understanding of which is essential if psychosocial interventions are to be implemented during recovery.

In this first section, stage and dimensional models of recovery will be reviewed together with a proposed model of recovery.

## THE PROCESS OF REINTEGRATION

### Theoretical models

Few prospective studies have systematically attempted to map the recovery process which follows an acute onset of schizophrenic symptoms. One notable exception is the study by Donlan and Blacker (1973) which suggests that patients pass through four distinct phenomenological stages during reintegration which are qualitatively the same as those passed through in decompensation, but in reverse order (for a more detailed review of stages of decompensation see Chapter 4). Donlan and Blacker carefully monitored 30 consenting out-patients several times per week over a period of eight weeks. During this time the patient's active medication was abruptly withdrawn, replaced by placebo for up to two weeks and then active medication reinstated. The patient was aware that during this time they may be placed on a non-active agent.

Full decompensation "psychic disorganisation and relief from subjective pain" (p. 202) was marked by less distressing auditory hallucinations and the formation of "compensatory" delusions. In the first stage, there was a withdrawal by the patient into their inner world which prohibited communication. The patient began to feel well but was totally lacking in insight. As reintegration progressed into the next stage subjective distress returned: painful memories and fears of loss of control invaded consciousness. The characteristic affects of this stage were those of panic, horror and fright. The next stage was predominantly marked by a depressive mood associated with loss of appetite, agitation and sleeplessness. The final stage of reintegration before recovery was typified by racing thoughts, anxiety, problems concentrating, feelings of vulnerability, frightening thoughts and dreams and low sexual drive. However, Donlan and Blacker found this progression through the four stages was not inevitable and could be arrested or even reversed if medication was sufficiently below a "therapeutic" dosage.

The limitation of this model, however, for clinical use is that many of the symptoms are explained in terms of psychodynamic theory with the qualitative and quantitative changes taking place in symptomology during the movement from one stage to another not clearly defined. Furthermore, there seems to be considerable overlap between stages.

Other stage theorists (e.g. Kayton, 1973 and Sachar et al., 1970) have also described four phases of reintegration, which although not directly comparable to Donlan and Blacker's stages, do show some resemblances. In Sachar et al. and Donlan and Blacker's models the first two stages of reintegration are concerned with the disintegration of core psychotic symptoms. For instance, Sacher et al. describe how a fixed delusional system in the first stage ("psychotic equilibrium") becomes unstable and fluid in the second stage ("acute psychotic turmoil") with delusions and ideas of reference readily formed but easily discarded. After stage 2 the symptoms described by both Donlan and Blacker and Sachar et al. are predominantly non-psychotic such as depression, anxiety, feelings of vulnerability and low self-esteem. Kayton (1973) devotes just one stage of his model "internal disorganisation" to the resolution of prominent psychotic symptoms but the post psychotic phases are described in more depth and detail than in the other models. For instance, the second stage "post psychotic regression" is marked by disturbed sleep and erratic eating patterns, impaired concentration and comprehension, social withdrawal and depression. The third stage "middle phase of post psychotic regression" is marked by return to normal sleeping and eating patterns with improved concentration and attention to grooming. Social interactions resume but are mainly non-verbal in nature. The fourth stage "termination of post psychotic regression" is marked by the patient taking pleasure in social interactions with a feeling of increased confidence and security. There is a return of ambition but goals are scaled down to realistic levels.

The concept of stages in recovery with the inherent theoretical assumption of boundaries and mutual exclusiveness has been criticised by Carr (1983). Many researchers suggest that the changes in symptomatology are best conceptualised as occurring on several independent dimensions. (Overall, Gorham and Shawver, 1961; Astrachan et al., 1974; Wittenborn, 1977; Dencker et al., 1978). Although these studies were conducted with a wide variety of sample sizes and types (e.g. chronic versus acute schizophrenic patients, those during a florid episode versus those some years into remission) along with different research aims, three groups of symptoms feature fairly consistently: psychoticism (e.g. disorganisation and distortion of thought process possibly with paranoia), retardation (e.g. reduced motor activity and lack of emotion) and dysphoria (e.g. anxiety, agitation and depression).

Carr (1983) has suggested a model whereby recovery can be monitored using five basic dimensions with a patient's position on each dimension not necessarily dependent on his/her position on the other dimensions. These dimensions are as follows:

1. *Psychotic disorganisation* which reflects the "internal disorganisation" described by Kayton (1973, 1975), "acute psychotic turmoil" described by Sachar et al. (1963, 1970) and "panic and horror" described by Donlan and Blacker (1973).

2. *Psychotic restitution* is concerned with the delusional state of the individual reflected in his or her conviction and preoccupation with delusional beliefs as well as the degree of implausibility or level of distortion of consensual reality. The term restitution reflects the individual's attempt to make sense of and adapt to a disturbing primary experience. This reduces anxiety and hence restores a degree of equanimity.

3. *Activation–inhibition* is a bipolar dimension with impulsivity and restlessness at one end versus anergia and withdrawal at the other.

4. *Neurotic restitution* is an attempt by the individual to adapt to dysphoric symptoms by non-psychotic means. A sense of equilibrium is achieved by directing attention away from agitation, low self-esteem, depression, etc towards various obsessions, phobias, compulsions and somatic complaints. (In Donlan and Blacker's study (1973), patients with obsessions and compulsions appeared less depressed.)

5. *Dysphoria* reflects the degree of subjective distress attributable to anxiety and depression. An individual may experience either anxiety and depression alternately or simultaneously. This model would certainly appear to have a great deal more flexibility than stage models whose

descriptions are not sufficiently comprehensive for clinical use. Also Carr's model is able to incorporate many of the findings of other empirical investigations (Overall, Gorham and Shawver, 1961; Astrachan et al., 1974; Dencker et al., 1978; Pious, 1961; Donlan and Blacker, 1973) and as such has face validity. However, even this model may not do justice to the complexity of changes that occur during recovery. For instance, the disintegration of delusions may be difficult to monitor due to their multi-dimensional character and the "marked de-synchrony and lack of covariance between different aspects of delusional beliefs". (Brett-Jones, Garety and Hemsley, 1987, p. 257).

In describing the changes that occur during recovery, neither stage nor dimensional models alone may be adequate for clinical use. Stage models are likely to be too restrictive and dimensional models cover any eventuality; with patients' positions on one dimension not predicting their position on another. It is suggested that a hybrid between these two models may be more useful—one of overlapping dimensions but with some distinct stages; for instance there may be an initial stage of psychotic disorganisation (with symptoms such as perceptual disturbance, tangentiality, distractibility, incongruity and incoherence of speech) before the other symptom clusters emerge, e.g. Sachar et al. (1963, 1970), Pious (1961). Dysphoric symptoms (particularly anxiety and depression) may be evident almost right through the course of recovery, but with some individuals a final stage may occur where only declining dysphoric symptoms are present, e.g. Donlan and Blacker (1973).

It is hypothesised that the patient's position on each of the dimensions are interdependent (Figure 2.1), for instance, the idea of psychotic restitution or delusion formation as a mastery process over frightening experiences is unlikely to occur until some of the mental chaos has abated. Disintegration of delusions may be related to the cessation of primary experiences such as depersonalisation although there may be a time lag between the two. Neurotic restitution, if it occurs, is likely to happen some time after the symptoms of psychotic disorganisation have subsided. Such a non-psychotic defence mechanism is unlikely to occur in a thought disordered and perceptually or affectively disturbed patient. However, this proposed model of recovery from an acute schizophrenic episode is all speculation with little data at present to support it. Further research involving prospective monitoring of recovering schizophrenic patients is therefore indicated to determine if there is an initial psychotic stage marked by an absence of delusional beliefs and non-psychotic symptoms; a final stage where only non-psychotic symptoms persist; and if the disintegration of delusions relate to changes in other symptom groups.

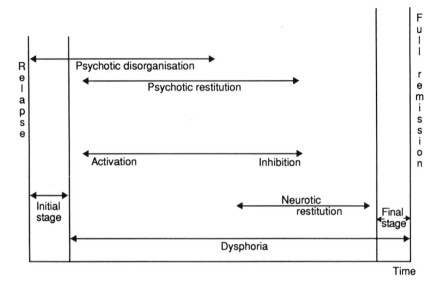

Figure 2.1  A proposed relationship between the five dimensions described by Carr (1983).

## Disintegration of delusional beliefs during recovery

Sacks, Carpenter and Strauss (1974) describe three stages in the recovery from delusional thinking. In the *delusional* phase the patient is totally immersed in his or her delusions to the point where what is thought and what is perceived is indivisible. This is followed by the *double awareness* phase where the patient can distance themselves from the delusion and can begin to reality test their beliefs and both accept and reject the beliefs. The patient "increasingly recognises the delusion as a symptom" (Sacks, Carpenter and Strauss, 1974, p. 119). In the final *non-delusional phase* there is an attempt to align the delusional ideas with reality; for instance, one patient who had grandiose delusions, when recovered rationalised that his feeling of great importance when ill was due to the fact that he knew his research data would be written up in textbooks (Sachs, Carpenter and Strauss, 1974). One patient who thought he was telepathic with his sister later rationalised the experience by saying "we are very close, we look alike maybe sometimes we think alike" (Early Signs Research Group, in preparation).

This, however, presents a rather over-simplified view of the changes that occur during the process of recovery from delusions. In a study of nine hospitalised schizophrenic patients, seen weekly soon after admission

(Brett-Jones, Garety and Hemsley, 1987) three key components of recovery from delusions were measured: degree of *conviction* in the belief; *preoccupation* with the belief (that is the amount of time spent thinking about the belief) and the degree to which the belief *interfered* with the everyday life of the individual. In support of the multi-dimensional view, seven of the nine subjects showed fluctuating scores on conviction and preoccupation with decreases in conviction tending to precede decreases in preoccupation. Correlations between conviction and preoccupation and conviction and interference, for the group of patients as a whole, were not significant (although the sample size was small) suggesting that these components are orthogonal dimensions.

Further evidence for the multi-dimensional view of delusions is reported in a study by Chadwick and Lowe (1990). Six clients who held fixed delusional beliefs for two or more years were monitored before, during and after two psychological interventions which consisted of a structured verbal challenge and a reality test. The data for individual clients showed a high degree of desynchrony between conviction, preoccupation and anxiety caused by thinking about the belief as the delusions receded. Many of the patients only sought out confirmatory evidence for their delusional beliefs rather than disconfirmatory objective experiences, which suggested to Brett-Jones, Garety and Hemsley (1987) that there are psychological processes involved in belief maintenance and disintegration which may not be unlike those involved in belief maintenance and decay in normal populations (Maher and Ross, 1984). This suggestion could have considerable significance for the prospects of accelerating recovery from an acute psychotic episode.

Many authors have suggested that some delusions are understandable when seen as an elaboration of, or a way of making sense of, an unusual set of perceptual experiences such as derealisation, depersonalisation and auditory hallucinations. This, however, does not explain *primary* delusions in which for example an individual suddenly becomes convinced that a set of events has special meaning: perhaps it is important to make the distinction between primary and secondary delusions when monitoring recovery. It is possible that patients holding secondary delusions are more likely to show a gradual but fluctuating decline in conviction during recovery as perceptions and beliefs about them are differentiated in the "double awareness" phase while primary delusions may disintegrate more abruptly. Such sudden shifts in conviction of primary delusions may be emotionally rather than cognitively based. In other words, the decline in conviction may not be due to the scrutiny and acknowledgement of objective events which are contrary to the belief but overwhelming *feelings* that the belief is false.

There are yet other delusions which would appear to be logically related and hence to show similar patterns of decline during recovery ("a domino effect"). For instance the secondary delusions "I am dead" (therefore) "I am rotting" (therefore) "I am infectious to children" would all appear to be inextricably linked. Similarly, the three delusions "I have cancer" (because) "I was drenched in Agent Orange" (because) "I fought in the Vietnam war" are obviously connected to one another.

The ability to "relabel delusions as pathological" is seen by David (1990) as an important component of insight. Consequently, as conviction in a delusional belief declines one might expect to see gains in insight.

### Non-psychotic symptoms and recovery

Non-psychotic symptoms including anxiety/agitation, depression/withdrawal, disinhibition and early psychotic thinking which herald a relapse of schizophrenia have been successfully monitored using early warning sign measures (Herz Early Signs Questionnaire 1985, Early Signs Scale (ESS), Birchwood, 1989). In a pilot study (Birchwood et al., 1989) carried out with 19 patients and observers over a 9 month period relapse was accurately predicted in 79% of cases using a cut-off point of 30 on their scale. Similar work, as yet unpublished, with recovering patients using this scale suggests that individuals display a mirror image decline in non-psychotic symptoms as recovery proceeds. Certain patients continue to show a decrease in non-psychotic symptoms after remission of positive symptoms which would be in line with those models of recovery that predict non-psychotic symptoms resolve at a later stage than psychotic symptoms: in a study by the Early Signs Research Group (in preparation), 79% of patients who achieved full or partial remission of positive symptoms (hallucinations and delusions) were scoring below the cut-off of 30 at the point of recovery (see Figures 2.2 and 2.3). Of all patients 66% were scoring less than 30 at the point of discharge. This finding would point to the usefulness of a simple cut-off point on the ESS for recovery as well as for relapse.

### Insight and recovery

If insight is conceptualised as simply an epiphenomenon of the presence or absence of acute psychopathology then one would assume insight to be low at relapse or just before admission to hospital and complete at recovery or remission of positive symptoms. In a study by McEvoy et al. (1989), however, "... degree of insight was not consistently related to the severity of acute psychopathology—nor did changes in insight during hospitalisation vary consistently with changes in acute psychopathology" (p. 43). It

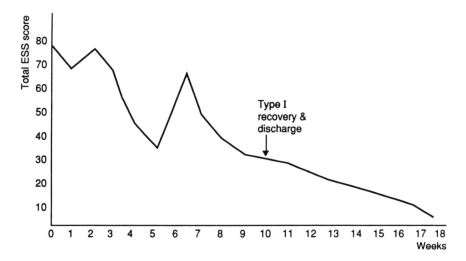

Figure 2.2 Changes in total ESS score during a type I recovery (full remission of positive symptoms).

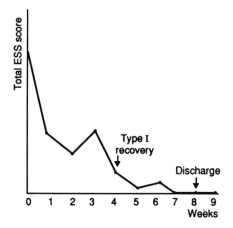

Figure 2.3 Changes in total ESS score during a type I recovery (full remission of positive symptoms).

is possible therefore that insight operates to some degree independently of symptomatology and may, in part, be dependent upon the individual's ability to reflexively examine his or her own experience—the way someone clinically depressed is able to say "I am depressed". In other words insight may require a psychological process. The concept of insight is according to David (1990) "composed of three distinct, overlapping dimensions". These are *treatment compliance, awareness of illness* and *correct relabelling of psychotic* experiences. If so, it is unlikely that in all patients insight will be low at relapse and high at recovery: need for treatment (i.e. to take medication, to be in hospital and to see a doctor) is partly a socially constructed concept and therefore may depend on the patients' attitude to the usefulness of drugs and medical intervention in general. David makes the distinction between "pseudo" and "true" insight. Pseudo insight relates to the regurgitation of psychiatric jargon without real understandings, e.g. "my delusions of grandeur are due to problems with the synapses in my brain". This phenomenon is perhaps only likely to be seen in patients with multiple admissions who have overheard explanations or have taken it on themselves to read psychiatric textbooks. Such utterances taken out of context of the patient's general behaviour and conversation would give a false indication of the level of a patient's insight.

In the study by the Early Signs Research Group (in preparation) insight was not found to be a binary phenomenon (see Figure 2.4), neither did it appear to be an inherent part of symptomatology as in some cases insight lagged behind the cessation of hallucinations and delusions (see Figure 2.4). In 37% of patients correct relabelling of psychotic experiences was either the last thing to be acknowledged or the only aspect never to be acknowledged. It may be that once primary experiences, e.g. auditory hallucinations and perceptual distortions have stopped and the vividness of the experience fades in the memory, it is easier to rationalise the experiences as being "all in the mind" and hence to be part of an "illness". This might also account for the time lag between the disappearance of positive symptoms and the achievement of full insight in some individuals. It

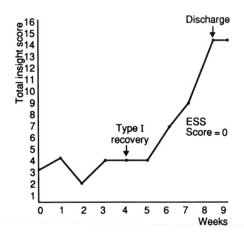

Figure 2.4  Gains in insight during type I recovery (full remission of positive symptoms).

does not explain, however, those patients who despite persistent auditory hallucinations readily accept the voices are "all in their mind", or conversely the patient whose delusions of reference from the TV have stopped many months previously but still holds total conviction they occurred in their past and explains it by saying "I'm not in dire straits anymore; I don't need the newsreader's help so they don't mention my name and give me advice now". Insight could therefore be a separate component of recovery as important as the positive symptoms themselves.

### The process of reintegration: conclusions

There are relatively few examples in the literature of prospective studies of recovery from acute psychosis (cf. Donlan and Blacker, 1973; Goldberg, Klerman and Cole, 1967; Bowers and Astrachan, 1967; Pious, 1961; Kayton, 1975; Sachar et al., 1963, 1970). Some of these studies can be criticised for relying too heavily on psychodynamic theory to explain observations and for the limitation of sample size (e.g. Pious used a single case study and Sachar et al. used a sample of four). Some theorists believe discrete stages adequately describe the process of reintegration (Donlan and Blacker, 1973), while others believe the recovery process is best conceptualised as occurring along several independent dimensions (Goldberg, Klerman and Cole, 1965). Although no homogeneous pattern of recovery emerges from these studies, differences in the rate and patterns of decline between symptom groups are often apparent; positive symptoms (e.g. hallucinations, delusions and thought disorder) tend to dominate the clinical picture in the early stages and can show an initial rapid and sharp decline, while negative symptoms (e.g. flattened affect, motor retardation) can either subside equally rapidly or show little change and hence predominate over residual positive symptoms. The decline in non-psychotic symptoms may show a more fluctuating pathway with a final stage of recovery in some individuals where only non-psychotic symptoms persist.

## PSYCHOSOCIAL INFLUENCES ON RECOVERY

Ward atmosphere and carers attitudes, i.e. the immediate psychosocial environments in which patients are involved, may play an important role in the recovery process. Kellam et al. (1967) found that wards with a low level of disturbed and aggressive behaviour along with a high degree of social interaction had a marked effect on the decline of paranoid symptoms but had little effect on symptoms of withdrawal. Admission wards with a high level of stress due to disruptive or violent behaviour of some patients could therefore extend rather than promote recovery in those patients where paranoia is a feature of symptomatology.

The concept of "expressed emotion" (EE) is a well established distal measure of interpersonal stress and has been operationalised in terms of the amount of hostility, over-involvement, and number of critical remarks elicited during the course of a factual interview with a carer about the patient (see Chapter 3). Schizophrenia patients with high EE relatives are more likely to relapse in nine months following discharge than those with low EE relatives (Brown, Birley and Wing, 1972).

It may be that those patients from high EE homes with relatives visiting on a regular basis will take longer to recover because of the higher levels of psychological stress they experience. Simpson (1989) considers the possibility that nurses "expressed emotion" may be a variable related to the recovery and outcome of schizophrenic patients.

A favourable convalescent environment defined as providing "a continuing feeling of safety but not hampering individualisation" (Kayton, Beck and Koh, 1976, p. 1271) and a therapeutic relationship defined as a "positive emotional engagement by patient and therapist in the context of help-giving" (Kayton, Beck and Koh, 1976, p. 1271), were both found to be significantly related to "good" outcome in 30 schizophrenic patients (Kayton, Beck and Koh, 1976). Sacks, Carpenter and Strauss (1974) postulate that a therapeutic relationship between researcher and patient may actually aid the recovery process "... he (the patient) is able to give as well as receive. The result is an increase in self-esteem and autonomy that encourages and fosters recovery" (p. 20).

It is suggested a period of convalescence (defined as the task of reintegration back into the community following the disruption of a psychotic episode) may last from a few weeks post discharge up to a full 12 months (Breier and Srauss, 1984). Breier and Strauss (1984) interviewed 20 patients who had been hospitalised for an acute psychotic episode, bi-monthly for one year post discharge. The extent to which social relationships with friends, family and spouse affected their symptoms, self-esteem and overall behaviour was investigated. Patients were asked to describe the most beneficial and most harmful aspects of these relationships. During convalescence, social relationships were seen to fulfil various helpful functions, in particular, ventilation of feelings, material support, help with problem solving, social approval and restoration of a sense of belonging.

During "rebuilding", a phase which follows convalescence and involves reducing reliance upon family and hospital and the cultivation of new friendships: motivation, symptom monitoring and participating as an equal partner in a reciprocal relationship were seen as most important.

The absence of a negative attitude rather than the presence of a very positive attitude towards their illness and the future was found to be associated with good outcome in 30 schizophrenic patients (McGlashan and Carpenter, 1981). Extrapolating from this finding, it may be that interventions to modify a patient's unrealistic positive or negative views about the effect of their illness on the future could have implications for recovery and prognosis. Romanticised positive attitudes of a quick return to normal functioning might prolong recovery if the patient is overwhelmed by depression when expectations are not met. Despairing negative attitudes about the illness might prolong recovery by preventing mobilisation of coping strategies to deal with residual symptoms.

## A PROCEDURE FOR MONITORING RECOVERY

The following is a procedure adopted by the Early Signs Research Group at All Saints and Barnsley Hall hospitals in Birmingham, UK and may be a model others wish to consider.

### Engagement

Patients should be approached preferably within two weeks of admission or relapse. It is important to stress confidentiality when explaining the purpose of monitoring as the process may be interpreted as further confirmatory evidence for any paranoid delusions that the patient may hold such as "the police are watching me and plotting against me", "the K.G.B. are after me".

A brief verbal explanation of the monitoring exercise should be given before commencement: "We are involved in monitoring the changes that occur in people's feelings and symptoms as they get better from their illness. The results from this exercise may help doctors to decide things like the best time for people to go home and the best time to reduce medication. We would like you to complete three questionnaires each week while in hospital and the same questionnaires every fortnight when you go home for about three months. The forms will be kept in your hospital notes and only those people involved with your care in hospital will have access to them".

There may be a problem with compliance especially as the monitoring involves the same questions repeated weekly. A good therapeutic relationship which has been nurtured between interviewer and patient is, however, likely to offset any tedium created by repetition as shown in a study by the Early Signs Research Group of 30 patients suffering from a relapse or first episode of schizophrenia where none of the patients withdrew their consent while in hospital and only one patient withdrew his consent after a period post discharge.

## Frequency and sources of information

Patients complete the phenomenological version of the Early Signs Scale (Birchwood et al., 1989) and an insight scale (Smith and Birchwood, 1991) weekly; in addition the Beliefs and Convictions Scale (Brett Jones, Garety and Hemsley, 1987) is completed weekly with an interviewer. An assessment of the mental state of a patient is made weekly by the interviewer using the Psychiatric Assessment Scale (PAS) (Krawiecka, Goldberg and Vaughn, 1977) and an independent assessment by a clinician is sought on admission, monthly and at discharge. An observer (e.g. a member of the nursing staff, relative or carer) is approached to complete the behavioural (observer) version of the Early Signs Scale. After discharge, for a period of approximately three months, patients and observers are asked to complete the same assessments fortnightly.

The procedure should therefore allow non-psychotic experiences which characterise recovery from an acute schizophrenic episode to be related to changes in psychotic phenomena, levels of insight and strength of delusional conviction.


## Standard measures

*The Psychiatric Assessment Scale* (Krawiecka, Goldberg and Vaughn, 1977)

This scale consists of eight categories of symptoms: depression, anxiety, hallucinations, delusions, flattened incongruous affect, psychomotor retardation, incoherence and irrelevance of speech and poverty of speech. The score for each category ranges from "0" where the item is for all practical purposes absent and "1" (mild) where there is some evidence for the item but it is not considered pathological; through to 2, 3 and 4 where the item is regarded as pathological ranging from moderate to severe. The rater decides on the severity of the item by taking into account the patients' demeanour and behaviour at interview as well as the history the patient gives. The scores for depression and anxiety are then summed together as are those for hallucinations and delusions (positive symptoms) and those for flattened affect and psychomotor retardation (negative symptoms) and those for incoherence and irrelevance of speech and poverty of speech (speech disorder).

The scores for depression and anxiety, positive symptoms, negative symptoms and speech disorder can be graphed separately each week (see Figure 2.5).


*Beliefs and convictions* (Brett-Jones, Garety and Hemsley, 1987)

Each belief is written down in the patient's own words e.g. "I believe my mother and father are aliens". A maximum of three beliefs are chosen in

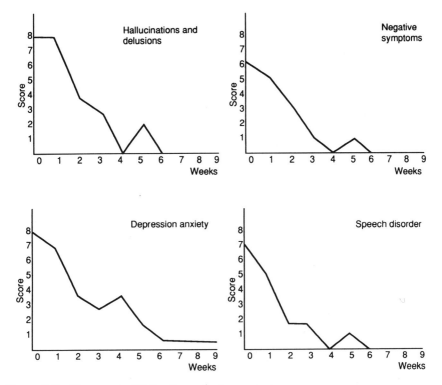

Figure 2.5   Changes in PAS ratings during recovery.

consultation with the patient and these are likely to be those interfering the most with the day-to-day functioning of the individual and/or causing the most anxiety.

Measures of *conviction* and *preoccupation* are elicited in two phases: a construction phase and an administration phase. A measure of *interference* that the belief has on the individual's day-to-day life is made by the interviewer: and a procedure to elicit reaction to hypothetical contradiction is administered.

*To determine the level of conviction.* In the construction phase, five statements of intensity of conviction are recorded in the patient's own words (with suggestions about intensity from the interviewer if necessary) e.g.:

There is very little chance that ... (statement of belief)
There is a slight chance that ...
I feel fairly sure that/there is a 50–50 chance that ...
I believe strongly that ...
I'm almost positive that ...

These are written on separate pieces of card and are ranked by the patient. In the administration phase, the cards are then presented to the patient separately in random order and the patient must say whether at the time of presentation they are more sure or less sure (about their belief) than the statement on the card.

The score (0–5) is equal to the number of cards to which the patient says his or her level of conviction is greater than that shown on the card.

*To determine degree of preoccupation.* As with conviction, patients choose five statements in their own words to represent the time they spend thinking about their belief, e.g.:

I hardly ever think about ... (statement of belief)
I think about ... (statement of belief) occasionally
I think about ... (statement of belief) some of the time
I think about ... (statement of belief) most of the time
I think about ... (statement of belief) nearly all the time

These are written on separate pieces of card and are individually presented to the patient in random order. The patient must say whether he or she thinks about his or her belief at the time of presentation more or less of the time than that indicated on the card.

The score (0–5) is equal to the number of cards to which the patients say their degree of preoccupation is greater than that shown on the card.

*To determine the degree of interference the belief has on the everyday life of the patient.* The rating is made by the interviewer on a 0–3 scale where:

0 is no interference,
1 is minor changes of behaviour are noted, e.g. can only listen to rather than watch TV, has to wear sunglasses indoors (to prevent people 'psyching' him out),
2 is disruption to normal hospital routine, e.g. cannot go to Day Centre, avoids TV room, laundry has to be washed separately from other patients' (as it is believed to be infectious),
3 is severe disruption to normal activities, e.g. cannot leave dormitory, cannot sit in day room when anyone else is present, cannot eat food from the hospital trolley, can only eat food brought in by relatives.

*Reaction to hypothetical contradiction.* The patient is given a hypothetical but plausible and concrete piece of evidence contradictory to his or her belief and asked how this affects the belief. This part of the scale is used to measure the individual's potential for accommodation of evidence incompatible with their belief as "... it may have some predictive value in picking out

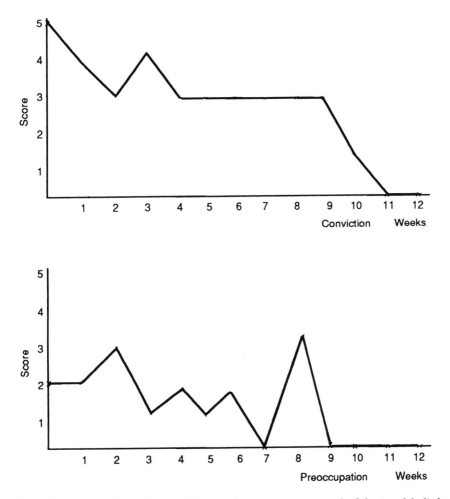

Figure 2.6   Fluctuations in conviction and preoccupation with delusional beliefs during recovery.

those most likely to make a complete recovery" (Brett-Jones, Garety and Hemsley, 1987, p. 264).

Replies are assigned to one of 4 categories:

1. The evidence is ignored or dismissed,
2. the evidence is accommodated into the belief system so that the belief and situation are now compatible, e.g. other people are able to eat the hospital food (which is poisoned) because they take a tablet on the way in,

3. there is a change in conviction but not content of the belief,
4. the belief is dropped.

The scores for preoccupation and conviction can be graphed separately each week (see Figure 2.6).

*Insight*

The Insight scale is one developed by Birchwood et al. (1992) and consists of eight statements (four negative and four positive) that the patients must either agree with, disagree with or say they are unsure about. The statements can be classified according to four subscales: the need for medication, the need to see a doctor or be in hospital, the acknowledgement of an illness and the relabelling of psychotic experiences.

The requisite agreement or disagreement with a statement scores 2 and a decision of unsure scores 1: the total score out of a maximum of 16 can be graphed weekly (see Figures 2.4 and 2.7). This scale has an advantage over some assessments (e.g. David, 1990) as it is a self-report and not an observer rating; so rendering an objective score rather than a subjective assessment by a rater.

*The Early Signs Scale (ESS)*

The ESS (Birchwood et al., 1989) is a randomly arranged checklist of 34 items describing feelings and behaviour known to occur in the period prior

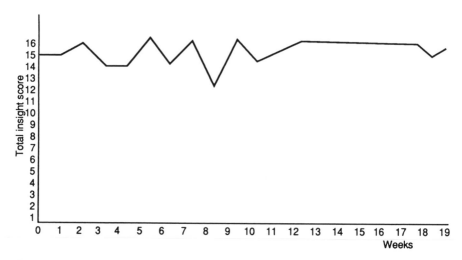

Figure 2.7   Changes in insight during recovery.

to relapse. Two versions of the scale are used: the self-report or pheno-menological version and the observer or behavioural version. The items of the scale measure aspects of symptomatology as follows: 6 items represent anxiety, 10 items represent negativity, 7 items represent disinhibition and 11 items represent incipient or early psychosis. Each item is self-rated on a scale of 0–3 where:

0 indicates the item has not occurred and is "not a problem",
1 indicates the item has occurred once a week and is a "little problem",
2 indicates the item has occurred several times a week but not daily and is a "moderate problem",
3 indicates the item has occurred at least once a day and is a "marked problem".

The total score and scores for anxiety, disinhibition, negativity and incipient psychosis are graphed weekly before discharge and fortnightly after discharge.

## Conducting the interviews

The interview should proceed as far as possible in a friendly atmosphere of mutual trust and respect with the emphasis on building up a rapport. Often there is a need to be "permission-giving" so individuals feel they can disclose symptoms without it having a detrimental effect on how people will react to them or on their length of stay in hospital. The approach should always be non-confrontational and non-judgemental with the interviewer adopting a reflective, non-directional style especially when discussing delusional beliefs.

It is preferable to complete the questionnaires in the order they have been described so that the ESS self-report does not confound the rater's judgement of the patient's mental state. For instance, the patient may report they have been reasonably cheerful all week, the future doesn't look too bad and their family have been to visit, which is congruous with their facial expression and general demeanour and yet when asked to complete the ESS item "feeling low or depressed" the patient reports this has occurred everyday. Obviously where patients are severely disturbed, aggressive, thought disordered or agitated, completion of the self-report questionnaires may prove difficult or impossible. Until the worst of these symptoms have abated it may only be possible to complete a Psychiatric Assessment Scale and to obtain an observers' version of the ESS.

## The Psychiatric Assessment Scale

Some of these ratings are best made using selected questions taken from the Present State Examination (Wing, Cooper and Sartorius, 1974) using modifications of the wording where appropriate. It is important when assessing positive symptoms that, as well as asking relevant global questions pertinent probes are used to "target" known delusions and hallucinations otherwise delusions, ideas of reference, etc may not be elicited: for example, in the case of a young woman who thought that the whole neighbourhood was gossiping about an "affair" with a neighbour's husband it was necessary to ask "how are you getting along with people at the moment ... with your family, friends and neighbours?" before an assessment of her delusional state could be made.

## The Beliefs and Convictions Scale

With the emphasis on a low-key, non-confrontational stance, gentle probes are made concerning the belief(s). No more than three beliefs are worked with at any one time and these are likely to be those causing the patient most distress or the ones he or she is most preoccupied with. The following example illustrates the eliciting of a belief that the patient's mother was a member of the KGB and shows the use of hypothetical contradictions.

*Eliciting the belief*

INTERVIEWER. Is there any particular worry or concern which is troubling you or on your mind a lot at the moment?
PATIENT. Everything is bothering me at the moment.
INTERVIEWER. Has your mother been to see you lately?
PATIENT. Yes, a couple of times this week.
INTERVIEWER. How are you getting along just now?
PATIENT. Dreadful.
INTERVIEWER. Why's that?
PATIENT. My mother is behaving very strangely.
INTERVIEWER. In what way is your mother behaving strangely?
PATIENT. She makes me cross when she goes round talking to the other patients—she's trying to psyche them out.
INTERVIEWER. How are you so sure she's trying to psyche them out?
PATIENT. Because she does it to me *and* she inserts thoughts into my head.
INTERVIEWER. How can she do these things?
PATIENT. Because she's a member of the secret police—she needs information.

*Eliciting the evidence*

The next stage attempts to elicit further evidence the patient has to support his belief:

INTERVIEWER. What makes you so sure your mother is a member of the secret police?
PATIENT. The things she does.
INTERVIEWER. What things in particular does your mother do which makes you suspect this?
PATIENT. My mother waits in the hospital car park until someone in a certain make of car leaves and then she follows them.
INTERVIEWER. Do you know why your mother does this?
PATIENT. She always drives close to the vehicle in front so she can read and memorise the number plate.
INTERVIEWER. Is there anything else your mother does which makes you suspect she's a member of the secret police?
PATIENT. Yes, she always brings items into the hospital concealed in two Tesco bags so no one can see what she is carrying ... when she leaves there is more in the bags than when she arrived. ... she has an evil glint in her eye and a malevolent smile.

*Hypothetical contradiction*

This information was met with the following hypothetical contradiction "just supposing an ex-member of the secret police were to tell you that your mother was too old and had inappropriate qualifications for the secret police would this lessen your worry at all?". The patient dismissed this hypothetical contradiction on the grounds that "ex-members wouldn't discuss secret police matters and if you were a member of the secret police you were a member for life". Sometime later when preoccupation but not conviction had decreased, the patient responded to the same hypothetical contradiction by saying his mother was "a lapsed or coerced member of the secret police".

It is important that the hypothetical contradictions are prefixed with statements like ... "just supposing ...", "how would you feel if ...", "some people are under the impression that ...", "some people say ...", so that the person does not feel their belief is under direct "fire" but rather a different point of view is being offered as a possible alternative.

It is also important to differentiate between hypothetical contradictions and verbal challenges. Both may be used in monitoring disintegration of delusional beliefs but only the latter is likely to aid the process of disintegration and therefore have therapeutic value as suggested by Chadwick and Lowe (1990).

To demonstrate the difference between hypothetical contradiction and verbal challenge consider a patient who believed he had AIDS. The belief was partly based on the patient's conviction that there was dirt on the needle the doctor had used to take a blood sample from him shortly after his admission. A hypothetical contradiction would be …"How would you feel if the same doctor came and saw you and reassured you he used a sterile, clean needle?". A verbal challenge would be "How would you feel knowing that only sterile needles are used in hospital. Needles are supplied to the ward pre-packed in sterile containers and are never re-used. Doctors and nurses are trained in the use of germ-free techniques and would wish to protect themselves. Does having this knowledge affect your belief at all?".

The latter is obviously factual information compared with the former which is simply supposition. Those patients who are willing to consider hypothetical contradictions and change their level of conviction in the light of them, even if only temporarily, are more likely to eventually drop their beliefs (Brett-Jones, Garety and Hemsley, 1987), and is thus a measure of their strength or fragility. It is the experience of the author that when working with floridly ill patients in this way it is preferable to keep the hypothetical contradictions as simple and as plausible as possible, otherwise convoluted ideas and propositions could only add to the mental chaos the patient may already be experiencing.

*Early Sign Scale*

Low self-report ESS scores may occur when insight is low and denial is occurring. This is to some extent compensated for by having an observer version but recruitment of observers on admission wards may be a problem especially where a key worker system does not operate. Reliability and validity may be compromised where numerous different raters, who do not confer, do not complete the questionnaire in consecutive weeks (for example due to holiday, sickness, etc.); or in cases where patients do not remain on the ward.

## MODAL PATTERNS OF RECOVERY

In a study by the Early Signs Research Group (in preparation) of 30 randomly selected in-patients suffering from either a relapse or a first episode of schizophrenia, three distinct categories of recovery were observed: type I was defined as complete remission of positive symptoms:

type II was defined as a partial remission of positive symptoms (a PAS score of ⩽4 when hallucinations and delusions are summed together): type III was defined as little or no change in ratings of positive symptoms; recovery in type III patients was denoted by a decrease in preoccupation with positive symptoms along with favourable behavioural changes.

Within each of these categories, however, different patterns could be detected. Some individuals (40%) showed a continuing decline in self-report ESS score (i.e. non-psychotic symptoms) after total remission or partial remission of positive symptoms (see Figure 2.2); while in others (20%) the ESS score showed no further decline (see Figure 2.8). Non-psychotic symptoms in this latter group of patients were extremely low by the time positive symptoms totally or partially remitted. It may be that the former group pass through a "convalescent" period in recovery roughly equivalent to the prodrome in relapse where the symptoms are predominantly non-psychotic in nature. This would tie in with Donlan and Blacker's stage theory but the problem is that the phenomenon does not appear to be universal. Carr's proposed dimensional model would allow for this discrepancy. If an individual's position on the psychotic disorganisation, psychotic restitution and dysphoria dimensions is not interdependent then dysphoric symptoms may remit simultaneously or at a later stage than positive symptoms. After full or partial remission of positive symptoms, some individuals (20%) showed an increase in nonpsychotic symptoms which coincided with a deterioration in mental state; this resulted in re-hospitalisation of all these individuals, except one who

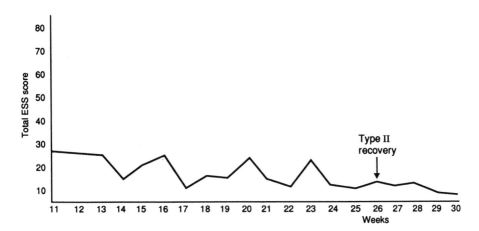

Figure 2.8   Changes in total ESS score during the latter stages of a type II recovery (partial remission of positive symptoms).

underwent "home treatment". In 48% of type I and type II recoveries a total ESS score of below 30 (in three consecutive weeks) for both observer and self-report was a good "rule of thumb" guide to recovery. Of all individuals 20% (predominantly type III recoveries) showed a pattern of fluctuating non-psychotic symptoms with a total ESS score which did not drop below 30; but tended to hover between 30 and 40 once preoccupation with positive symptoms had decreased.

In line with Brett-Jones, Garety and Hemsley (1987) and Chadwick and Lowe (1990) delusional conviction and preoccupation were found to fluctuate independently. Decreases in preoccupation tended to precede decreases in conviction (see Figure 2.6) which is in contrast to the finding of Brett-Jones, Garety and Hemsley (1987) that decreases in conviction preceded decreases in preoccupation. In some cases where delusions remained fixed, preoccupation was the only variable to change. Insight appeared to be inconsistently related to degree of illness as found by McEvoy et al. (1989). Of the 30 patients monitored by the Early Signs Research Group 16 showed a pattern of high insight (score >12) at commencement of monitoring with high insight at discharge; and ten of these 16 patients were seen in the first week after admission (see Figure 2.7). Twelve patients showed a gradual increase in insight during recovery: four of these showed a pattern of low insight (score <6) at commencement of monitoring changing to high insight at discharge; and five patients showed a pattern of low insight at commencement of monitoring and moderate insight at discharge. Two patients showed little change in their low level of insight which was consistent with little change in positive symptoms.

Relabelling of psychotic experiences was the last aspect of insight to show change in over a third of patients; change in other components of insight showed a desynchronous pattern. Fluctuations in insight of first episode patients appeared to be related to "denial" and "coming to terms with the illness". Attitudes of first episode patients towards medication, seeing a doctor and hospitalisation appeared to vacillate much more than patients suffering from a relapse of schizophrenia. Most first episode patients refused to accept their diagnosis and expressed the need to test out the validity of the diagnosis by stopping their medication to see if the illness would return. Patients actively sought out less stigmatising explanations for their symptoms such as stress, abuse of drugs and their upbringing. Taylor and Perkins (1991) suggest denial of the illness may be likened to the denial stage in the ongoing process of grieving after a bereavement whereby disturbing emotions are temporarily refused access to consciousness until more demanding coping strategies such as acceptance can be adopted.

## PSYCHOSOCIAL INTERVENTIONS TO PROMOTE RECOVERY FROM ACUTE PSYCHOSIS

### Rationale

Recent successes with cognitive behavioural interventions for refractory delusions (Chadwick and Lowe, 1990) and drug-resistant auditory hallucinations (Chadwick and Birchwood, in press), alongside the fact that normal psychological processes appear to prevail during maintenance and disintegration of delusional beliefs (Brett-Jones, Garety and Hemsley, 1987) such that acting on a delusion may be a test of corroboration or disconfirmation (Buchanan et al., 1993), suggest that cognitive therapy may be effective in reducing positive symptoms during an acute episode. The stress vulnerability model (Neuchterlein and Dawson, 1984; Neuchterlein, 1987) and research concerning expressed emotion (Leff and Vaughn, 1988) proposes that certain environmental stressors such as an intolerant family climate may precipitate psychotic relapse, and by inference such environmental stressors may hinder recovery.

Some ward atmospheres have been found to have an effect on recovery and outcome. Calm but sociable wards were found to be advantageous for the recovering patient (Kellam et al., 1967), as were highly structured wards aimed at reducing environmental chaos (Raskis, 1960), whilst unstimulating, deprived social milieus were found to increase negative symptoms (Wing and Brown, 1970). Therefore, it would appear that by reducing stressful interactions and providing purposeful activity involving reciprocal relationships, the recovery process may be enhanced.

Other research indicates that the recovery process is likely to be managed most effectively if the individual can be made aware of their active role in coping with the illness (McGorry, 1992; Strauss, 1992), if their strengths can be harnessed to bring about a process of change and personal growth that can protect them from the damaging effects of stigma (Davidson and Strauss, 1992) and when the individual's conflicts and needs so often manifested in florid symptomatology have been addressed. Patients who are able to find personal significance in their psychotic experiences and can "integrate" them into a wider view of themselves and the world appear to benefit from the process (McGlashan, Levy and Carpenter, 1974).

It is proposed, therefore, that the length of exposure to florid psychosis may be reduced by asking patients to engage in an intervention that has two main themes: a cognitive approach to symptom management with an emphasis on acceptance and mastery of the illness, and the provision of a milieu with optimal stimulation and minimal stressful interaction.

The Birmingham recovery project has (at the time of writing) recently been completed and the intervention consists of four psychosocial procedures:

1. Individual cognitive therapy in the context of a supportive relationship, which involves eliciting evidence for delusional beliefs, including those linked to auditory hallucinations, with subsequent challenging of that evidence in reverse order of importance to the belief. This is conducted in an atmosphere of "collaborative empiricism" as described by Chadwick and Lowe (1990), Chadwick (in press) and Chadwick and Birchwood (in press). This is followed up by an empirical test of the belief, where appropriate.
2. Group cognitive therapy methods in the context of education about the aetiology, nature and treatment of psychotic illness. This is a manoeuvre to promote "universality" and to challenge beliefs by observing the inconsistencies and the way in which others' beliefs hold together. Considerable emphasis is given to empowerment of patients through identifying and exchanging ideas about helpful coping strategies for both negative and positive symptoms, by teaching stress management techniques and by specifying ways to avoid or cope with impending relapse. Patients are greatly encouraged to try and "face up" to their illness rather than seeking refuge back in their psychotic experiences.
3. Family education and support conducted with one family at a time, in an attempt to respond to individual family needs and to reduce family intolerance of difficult behaviour, family anxiety and family impatience for a quick solution or "cure". Specific guidance is given with regard to helpful ways of interacting with the patient during the acute episode and how to help the patient manage the symptoms.
4. A meaningful activity programme in a relaxed atmosphere away from the ward designed to reduce negative symptoms, to encourage social networking and improve self-esteem.

**A study to promote recovery**

Fifty-eight acutely ill patients with a clinical diagnosis of non-affective psychosis were selected randomly from the acute wards of an inner city psychiatric hospital. In addition to routine service provision, 20 patients were asked to engage in the psychosocial intervention for 8–10 h per week, 20 patients were asked to engage in monitoring and recreational pursuits away from the ward for a matched number of hours, and the remaining 18 received weekly minimal monitoring of their symptomatology. Each patient was seen weekly and assessments of their mental state, insight, conviction in and preoccupation with delusional beliefs and non-psychotic signs were made as described previously.

Table 2.1 Outcome of patients receiving intervention compared with recreational activity controls: provisional data

|  | Intervention ($n = 20$) | Control ($n = 20$) |
| --- | --- | --- |
| Mean days to "recovery" | 65 | 124[*] |
| Mean days in hospital | 56 | 122[†] |
| Early relapse or readmission | 15% | 35% |
| Full remission of positive symptoms | 65% | 40% |
| *Engagement with services at follow-up*[‡] |  |  |
| Contact with services[§] | 81% | 67% |
| Medication compliance | 94% | 56% |
| Prevocational training or in |  |  |
| employment | 50% | 33% |

[*] $P < 0.016$.
[†] $P < 0.037$.
[‡] Control group figures based on sample ($n = 10$) because some patients still in follow-up period.
[§] Services include out-patient appointments, contact with Community Mental Health Team and/or community psychiatric nurse and attendance at day centres.

Preliminary data available at the time of writing suggest that patients receiving the intervention achieve significantly shorter and qualitatively different recoveries to those receiving recreational activities and routine service provision, and 65% of those in the intervention group achieved a full recovery or complete remission of positive symptoms compared with 40% in the recreational activity control group (see Table 2.1). Furthermore, those in the intervention group were more likely to have ongoing involvement with services, had taken advantage of prevocational training or were working, and more were compliant with medication and avoided readmission and relapse.

## Acknowledgement

The Early Signs Research Group would like to thank Research and Development for Psychiatry for their support in funding the study on recovery discussed in this chapter.

## REFERENCES

Astrachan, B.M., Brauer, L., Harrow, M. and Schwartz, C. (1974) Symptomatic outcome in schizophrenia. *Archives of General Psychiatry*, **31**, 155–60.
Birchwood, M. (1989) Early Signs Scale (personal communication).
Birchwood, M., Smith, J., Macmillan, F., Hogg, B., Prasad, R., Harvey, C. and Bering, S. (1989) Predicting relapse in schizophrenia: the development and

implementation of an early signs monitoring system using patients and families as observers. *Psychological Medicine*, **19**, 649–56.

Birchwood, M., Smith, J., Drury, V., Healy, J. and Slade, M. (1994) A self-report insight scale for psychosis: reliability, validity and sensitivity to change. *Acta Psychiatrica Scandinavica*, **89**, 62–7.

Birchwood, M., Cochrane, R., Macmillan, F., Copestake, S., Kucharska, J. and Cariss, M. (1992) The influence of ethnicity and family structure on relapse in first episode schizophrenia: a comparison of Asian, Caribbean and white patients. *British Journal of Psychiatry*, **161**, 783–90.

Bowers, M.B. Jr. and Astrachan, B.M. (1967) Depression in acute schizophrenic psychosis. *American Journal of Psychiatry*, **123**, 976–9.

Brett-Jones, J., Garety, P. and Hemsley, D. (1987) Measuring delusional experiences: a method and its application. *British Journal of Clinical Psychology*, **26**, 257–65.

Breier, A. and Strauss, J.S. (1984) The role of social relationships in the recovery from psychotic disorders. *American Journal of Psychiatry*, **141**, 949–55.

Brown, G.W., Birley, J.L.T. and Wing, J.K. (1972) The influence of family life on the course of schizophrenia: a replication. *British Journal of Psychiatry*, **121**, 241–58.

Buchanan, A., Reed, A., Wessely, S., Garety, P., Taylor, P., Grubin, D. and Dunn, G. (1993) Acting on delusions. II: The phenomological correlates of acting on delusions. *British Journal of Psychiatry*, **163**, 77–81.

Carr, V.J. (1983) Recovery from schizophrenia: a review of patterns of psychosis. *Schizophrenia Bulletin*, **9**, 95–121.

Chadwick, P. A cognitive approach to measuring and modifying delusions. *Behaviour Research and Therapy* (in press).

Chadwich, P. and Birchwood, M. Challenging the omnipotence of voices: a cognitive approach to auditory hallucinations. *British Journal of Psychiatry*, **164**, 190–201.

David, A.S. (1990) Insight and psychosis. *British Journal of Psychiatry*, **156**, 798–808.

Davidson, L. and Strauss, J. (1992) Sense of self in recovery from severe mental illness. *British Journal of Medical Psychology*, **65**, 131–45.

Dencker, S.J., Frankenberg, K., Lepp, M., Lindberg, D. and Malm, U. (1978) How schizophrenic patients change during 3 years' treatment with depot neuroleptics. *Acta Psychiatrica Scandinavica*, **57**, 115–23.

Donlan, P.T. and Blacker, K.H. (1973) Stages of schizophrenic decompensation and reintegration. *Journal of Nervous and Mental Disease*, **157**, 200–9.

Goldberg, S.C., Klerman, G.L. and Cole, J.O. (1965) Changes in schizophrenic psychopathology and ward behaviour as a function of phenothiazine treatment. *British Journal of Psychiatry*, **111**, 120–33.

Herz, M.I. (1985) Early Signs Questionnaire (personal communication).

Kayton, L. (1973) Good outcome in young adult schizophrenia. *Archives of General Psychiatry*, **29**, 103–10.

Kayton, L. (1975) Clinical features of improved schizophrenics. In: Gunderson, J.G. and Mosher, L.R. (eds), *Psychotherapy of Schizophrenia*, Jason Aronson, New York.

Kayton, L., Beck, J. and Koh, S.D. (1976) Post-psychotic state, convalescent environment and the therapeutic relationship in schizophrenic outcome. *American Journal of Psychiatry*, **133**, 1269–74.

Kellam, S.G., Goldberg, S.C., Schooler, N.R., Berman, A. and Shmelzer, J.L. (1967) Ward atmosphere and outcome of treatment of acute schizophrenia. *Journal of Psychiatric Research*, **5**, 145–63.

Krawiecka, M., Goldberg, D. and Vaughn, M. (1977) Standardised psychiatric assessment scale for chronic psychiatric patients. *Acta Psychiatrica Scandinavica*, **36**, 25–31.

Leff, J. and Vaughn, C. (1988). *Expressed Emotion in Families*, Guilford Press, New York.

Maher, B. and Ross, J.S. (1984) Delusions. In: H.E. Adams and P. Sutker (eds), *Comprehensive Handbook of Psychopathology*, Plenum, New York.

McEvoy, J.P., Apperson, L.J., Applebaun, P.S., Ortlip, P., Brecosky, J., Hammill, K., Geller, J.L. and Roth, L. (1989) Insight in schizophrenia: its relationship to acute psychopathology. *Journal of Nervous and Mental Disease*, **177**, 43–7.

McGlashan, T.H. and Carpenter, W.T. Jr. (1981) Does attitude towards psychosis relate to outcome? *American Journal of Psychiatry*, **138**, 797–801.

McGlashan, T., Levy, S. and Carpenter, W. (1975) Integration and sealing over clinically distinct recovery styles from schizophrenia. *Archives of General Psychiatry*, **32**, 1269–72.

McGorry, P. (1992) The concept of recovery and secondary prevention in psychotic disorders. *Australia and New Zealand Journal of Psychiatry*, **26**, 3–17.

Neuchterlein, K. (1987) Vulnerability models for schizophrenia: state of the art. In: Hafner, H., Gattaz, W., Janarzik, W. (eds), *Search for Causes of Schizophrenia*, Springer, Berlin.

Neuchterlein, K. and Dawson, M. (1984) A heuristic vulnerability—stress model of schizophrenia episodes. *Schizophrenia Bulletin*, **10**, 300–12.

Overall, J.E., Gorham, D.R. and Shawver, J.R. (1961) Basic dimensions of change in the symptomatology of chronic schizophrenics. *Journal of Abnormal and Social Psychology*, **63**, 597–602.

Pious, W.L. (1961) A hypothesis about the nature of schizophrenic behaviour. In: A. Burton (ed.), *Psychotherapy of the Psychoses*, pp. 43–68, Basic Books, New York.

Raskis, H. (1960) Cognitive restructuring: why research is therapy. *Archives of General Psychiatry*, **2**, 612–21.

Sachar, E.J., Mason, J.W., Kolmer, H.S. and Artiss, K.L. (1963) Psychoendocrine aspects of acute schizophrenic reactions. *Psychosomatic Medicine*, **25**, 510–37.

Sachar, E.J., Kanter, S.S., Buie, D., Engle, R. and Mehlman, R. (1970) Psycho-endocrinology of ego disintegration. *American Journal of Psychiatry*, **125**, 1076–8.

Sacks, M.H., Carpenter, W.T. Jr. and Strauss, J.S. (1974) Recovery from delusions: three phases documented by patients interpretations of research procedures. *Archives of General Psychiatry*, **30**, 117–20.

Simpson, R.B.C. (1989) Expressed emotion and nursing the schizophrenic patient. *Journal of Advanced Nursing*, **14**, 459–66.

Smith, J. and Birchwood, M. (1990) Relatives and patients as partners in the management of schizophrenia. *British Journal of Psychiatry*, **156**, 654–60.

Strauss, J. (1992) The person—key to understanding mental illness: towards a new dynamic psychiatry, 111. *British Journal of Psychiatry*, **161** (suppl. 18), 19–26.

Taylor, K.E. and Perkins, R.E. (1991) Identity and coping with mental illness in long stay psychiatric rehabilitations. *British Journal of Clinical Psychology*, **30**, 73–85.

Wing, J. and Brown, G. (1970). Institutionalism and schizophrenia: a comparative study of 3 mental hospitals 1960–1968, Cambridge University Press, London.

Wing, J.K., Cooper, J.E. and Sartorius, N. (1974) Measurement and classification of psychiatric symptoms. An instruction manual for the PSE and Catego Program, Cambridge University Press, London.

Wittenborn, J.R. (1977) Stability of symptom ratings for schizophrenic men. *Archives of General Psychiatry*, **34**, 437–40.

Chapter 3

# Interventions with Families

CHRISTINE BARROWCLOUGH AND
NICHOLAS TARRIER

## INTRODUCTION

Research programmes designed to assist families in coping with a family member suffering from schizophrenia have generated considerable interest over the last decade. The aims of this chapter are to review the research on these intervention studies and to provide practical guidelines to those who may wish to implement them.

The idea that family environments have a causative role in schizophrenia and the subsequent application of family therapy as a treatment method has a long history (see Falloon, Boyd and McGill, 1984). However, the iatrogenic effects of such family pathology models have now been well documented (Terkelson, 1983; Lefley,1989). In recent years the focus of interest has shifted to the role of family environments in precipitating relapses in vulnerable individuals who have already experienced an episode of schizophrenia: that is, the importance of the domestic environment in the course rather than the aetiology of the illness. If factors in the patient's environment could be identified as contributing to relapse, then in theory, these factors could be modified and relapse prevented. This has been the rationale for family intervention studies.

## EARLY INTERVENTIONS STUDIES

Early studies of family interventions were unsuccessful in reducing relapse rates. For example, Hogarty and his colleagues carried out two large scale studies which examined the effects of neuroleptic medication and social case work on relapse (Hogarty et al., 1974a, 1974b, 1979), but neither of these studies reported convincing evidence for the efficacy of the interventions. Similar negative findings were reported by Hudson (1975) and

Cheek et al. (1971) using operant techniques, although these programmes were somewhat over-simplistic in their conception. The first successful report in favour of family intervention was that by Goldstein et al. (1978) on the use of crisis oriented family therapy. Goldstein and co-workers randomly allocated 104 young first or second episode schizophrenic patients to either moderate or low dose medication and to either psycho-social intervention or standard aftercare. After six weeks there were significant differences in readmission rates for the high dose plus family therapy group (0%) compared to the low dose and standard care (24%). After six months there were still no re-admissions in the high dose and family therapy group. A more recent study comparing family education with family problem solving carried out in a group format found no significant difference in relapses between the two treatments (Ehlert, 1989).

## CONTROLLED STUDIES OF FAMILY INTERVENTION BASED ON EE AS A RISK FACTOR

The main impetus for family interventions has been the research on Expressed Emotion (EE). It has been demonstrated in a large number of studies that this index is a remarkably robust predictor of schizophrenic relapse, at least in the short term. Since patients who are discharged into households where a relative is rated high on EE have significantly higher relapse rates, the measure has been viewed not only as a risk factor, but as an explanatory variable in relapse. However, little is known about how EE—essentially a measure of verbal report and tone of voice—translates into a mechanism for relapse in the home environment. From a treatment viewpoint this poses some problems: if the precise nature of stressful inter-actions in the patient's home cannot be identified, how does one target behaviours for change? In practice, certain assumptions have been made about the kind of problems or deficits associated with high EE families which may contribute to stressful environments: these include misunder-standings about the illness resulting in conflict or unrealistic expectations of the patient; and difficulties with problem solving, communication or coping skills. Interventions have been designed to address these problems, thus reducing EE or ameliorating other sources of stress within the family. These studies are briefly reviewed below, with particular attention directed at outcome measure issues.

### Relapse

Most studies have focused on relapse rates as the main outcome measure. The relapse rates achieved by the intervention studies which have targeted high EE families as a high risk group are presented in Table 3.1. Four of these studies demonstrated that family interventions significantly reduced relapse rates when compared to control groups (Falloon et al., 1982; Leff et al., 1982; Hogarty et al., 1986; Tarrier et al., 1988), and a common characteristic of these programmes was the inclusion of both the relative and the patient in the treatment strategies.

Table 3.1   Relapse rates in percentages for high EE households from published Family Intervention studies. Percentages in parentheses represent "treatment takers" only and exclude those who did not complete the intervention programme

| Study | Relapse rates (%) 9 or 12 months | 24 months |
|---|---|---|
| Camberwell Study 1 (Leff et al., 1982, 1985) | | |
| Family intervention | 8 | 20 |
| Routine treatment | 50 | 78 |
| Camberwell Study 2 (Leff et al., 1989, 1990) | | |
| Family therapy | 8 | 33 |
| Relatives groups | 17 | 36 |
| California-USC Study (Falloon et al., 1982, 1985) | | |
| Family intervention | 6 | 17 |
| Individual intervention | 44 | 83 |
| Hamburg Study (Kottgen et al., 1984) | | |
| Group psychodynamic intervention | 33 | |
| Control group | 43 | |
| Pittsburgh Study (Hogarty et al., 1986, 1987) | | |
| Family intervention | 23 (19) | (32) |
| Social skills training | 30 (20) | (42) |
| Combined FI & SST | 9 (0) | (25) |
| Control group | 41 | 66 |
| Salford Study (Tarrier et al., 1988, 1989) | | |
| Family intervention | 12 (5) | 33 (24) |
| Education programme | 43 | 57 |
| Routine treatment | 53 | 60 |
| Sydney Study (Vaughan et al., 1991a) | | |
| Relatives' counselling | 41 | |
| Control group | 65 | |

Two studies—the Hamburg (Kottgen et al., 1984) and the Sydney (Vaughan et al., in press (a)) studies—failed to demonstrate a significant reduction in relapse. However, these programmes differed in the nature of their interventions when compared to the four successful ones noted above. The Hamburg study has been criticised on methodological grounds (Vaughn, 1986a); also it was psychoanalytic in orientation, was conducted in a group format, and treated patients and relatives separately. The Sydney study focused solely on the relatives and the research team never saw the patients. A considerable number of patients (58%) were not on medication after discharge, in contrast to the successful studies where medication compliance was good. Furthermore, the research team did not liaise with the team responsible for the patients' clinical management and the intervention itself was relatively short (ten weekly sessions). One other study carried out by Leff and his colleagues (Leff et al., 1989) also focused on the relatives alone, and the results indicated that attending relatives' groups was equivalent to individual family therapy, but the drop-out rate in the relatives' groups was very high and the low subject numbers make the results of this study difficult to interpret. Finally, one study has included a patient-only focused intervention. Hogarty et al. (1986) found that, at least over the first 12 months after discharge, social skills training with the patient alone was equivalent to family management in terms of relapse rates.

Comparisons in the other studies indicate that short educational programmes are ineffective (Tarrier et al., 1988); and that prolonged intervention after the first year prevents relapses proliferating in the second year (Falloon et al., 1985).

From the findings of these studies it is possible to produce a number of guidelines for effective interventions for relapse reduction:

1. Intervention should focus on both relatives and patients in the family unit, but individual intervention with the patient will also be beneficial,
2. Education alone is insufficient, but may be useful as part of a more extensive programme of assistance,
3. Interventions should be maintained over an extended period of time,
4. Interventions should take place in liaison with other aspects of the patient's management, and preferably be integrated with the established mental health services,
5. Intervention should also attempt to maintain medication compliance.

A number of other studies are presently being carried out, although the results from these are not yet available. Of special interest are studies such as the NIMH Collaborative Study and the Munich study which examine the interaction of family management with medication regimes. Why interventions work to reduce relapse is a critical question. All workers in the area have emphasised the importance of stress and stressful home environments but the precise nature of the stressful stimuli in the home have yet to be identified. A series of studies have attempted to examine the effects of the relatives' EE levels on the patients' arousal levels (see Turpin, Tarrier and Sturgeon, 1988; Dawson, Liberman and Mintz, 1989; Tarrier, 1989 for reviews). Although the results of these studies are not completely clear, they suggest that, especially during an acute episode, patients who have been living with a high EE relative have high levels of background tonic arousal and a hyperreactivity to the direct presence of their relative. These psychophysiological studies allow us to produce a tentative explanation of how interventions work. Stressful environments, whether they be in the family home or elsewhere, result in an accumulating increase in the patient's underlying tonic arousal and a hyperreactivity to certain social and environmental stimuli. If this hyperaroused state does not habituate then eventually a threshold is reached and symptoms reappear. This is presumably because high arousal disrupts perceptual processes and information processing capacities. Environments are likely to be stressful when they are complex, unpredictable, ambiguous and emotionally charged, such as living with a critical, hostile or over-involved relative. Interventions will be successful if they decrease the complexity, ambiguity and emotionality and increase the predictability and clarity of the environment. However, it is likely that future research may further refine these hypotheses. There is already some evidence from the literature that criticism and hostility are more predictive of relapse than marked emotional overinvolvement (Hogarty et al., 1986; Vaughan et al., 1991b) and certainly criticism is the more common dimension to score above the high EE threshold in study samples (Vaughn, 1986b). It may be that EE is a binary rather than unitary concept and some aspects of relatives' behaviour included in the high EE classification could present greater stress or problems for patients than other behaviours: for example, coercion may be more stressful than intrusion.

## Multiple outcome measures

Although relapse has been the key outcome variable in intervention studies, multiple measures of outcome are more appropriate for assessing the efficacy of work with families (Barrowclough and Tarrier, 1984; Smith and Birchwood, 1990). Some studies have attempted to report other such measures.

*Social functioning*

Both the California (Falloon, Boyd and McGill, 1984) and Salford (Barrow-clough and Tarrier, 1990) studies systematically measured the patient's level of social functioning. Both studies found that patients in the family intervention groups showed significant increases compared to control groups. Leff et al. (1989) reported small but non-significant increases in anecdotal reports on social functioning in patients receiving interventions.

*Relatives' burden*

There is evidence to suggest that relatives carry a considerable burden in caring for the mentally ill (Creer and Wing, 1974; Fadden, Kuipers and Bebbington, 1987). Controlled trials of community care versus traditional care have not shown a reduction in family burden in the former (Test and Stein, 1980; Reynolds and Hoult, 1984) and there is concern that increasing moves to implement community care and family management will result in extra burden on the family. Falloon and his colleagues (Falloon and Pederson, 1985) have attempted to address this issue. They found decreases in relatives' subjective burden, social and clinical morbidity and increases in family coping behaviour for families receiving family intervention. The authors suggested that these improvements resulted from decreases in positive symptoms and disruptive behaviour in the study patients.

*Consumer satisfaction*

The acceptability of family interventions by the "consumers" or service recipients is an important but frequently ignored variable. This is impor-tant both because it reflects on the quality of the service but also because of a backlash against psychosocial research (e.g. Hatfield, 1987), given that families have at best been implicated in the poor prognosis of patients and at worst blamed for causing schizophrenia. In the Salford study all rela-tives reported that they were at least "fairly satisfied" with the intervention, and 88% said they were "extremely satisfied". Similarly, 75% indicated that the specific help they had received had been "extremely helpful". This was so even when the relatives did not necessarily feel optimistic about the patients' future recovery.

*Economic considerations*

Economic factors are becoming increasingly more important in the plan-ning of health services. It is no longer sufficient for the researcher to dem-onstrate the clinical efficacy of their intervention. The economic viability must also be proven. Of the intervention studies described, two attempted some type of economic analysis. Falloon and his colleagues (Cardin, McGill and Falloon, 1986) undertook a detailed analysis of all direct and indirect costs to the patients, families, health, welfare and community agencies associated with their intervention. A cost-benefit analysis of the twelve month data showed the total costs for family management were 19% less than for individually managed patients (Cardin, McGill and Falloon, 1986). A much less ambitious analysis of the Salford project was undertaken by Tarrier, Lowson and Barrowclough (1991), and only direct costs were analysed. The treatment of patients who received family intervention showed an overall saving of 37% over the high EE control groups, and a saving of 27% on mean per patient costs. In both these studies reducing in-patient days was a big factor in reducing costs.

## Working with the families of schizophrenic patients: some practical guidelines

We have emphasised the fact that there are aspects of the relationship between schizophrenic relapse and the behaviour of relatives which are poorly understood. "High EE" relatives are a heterogeneous group, representing a range of problems, coping styles and interaction patterns as well as unique strengths and assets. Thus there are no "cookbook" answers as to the most important targets for behaviour change in relatives, and packages of techniques are premature and inappropriate. Additionally, a cause and effect model of EE and schizophrenic relapse is over simplistic, and it would be unfortunate if therapists adopted such a viewpoint. Illness factors—chronicity and severity of symptoms including behavioural disturbances—may well contribute to the development of problems in families and in difficulties in managing behaviour. Moreover, it is misleading to conceptualise all low EE relatives as calm, effective copers who facilitate rehabilitation and reduce the risk of relapses by creating a stress free domestic atmosphere. Given the severe and pervasive consequences of the illness, one should not assume that any relative of a schizophrenia sufferer is without difficulties; and it has been suggested that a lack of marked criticism or over involvement may sometimes be a function of "burn out" with the distancing of the relative from the patient's problems (Vaughn, in press (b)), or that relapse reduction in low EE homes may be at the cost of reduced social functioning (Birchwood and Smith, 1987). Additionally, it has been suggested that low EE relatives may develop "high EE behaviours" if the patient deteriorates.

These considerations indicate that training in EE assessments is not a necessary prerequisite for working with the families and a "needs led" rather than "EE reduction" approach is more appropriate for clinical practice. Moreover, there should be multiple measures of treatment efficacy and focusing on relapse prevention may obscure the needs of individual families. However, some understanding of the EE measure is helpful in providing a framework for evaluating coping strategies and in pointing to areas of possible need. The Salford intervention study adopted an approach whereby the individual needs of family members were assessed while knowledge about EE informed the therapists' framework for setting priorities for behaviour change. The following guidelines are derived from the study's intervention format.

## INITIAL ASSESSMENTS

A comprehensive and detailed assessment of the individual and collective needs of family members is essential to successful intervention with the family. This should be a collaborative exercise whereby the therapists assist the family to express and clarify their difficulties, as well as highlighting their strengths and resources. It is useful to see family members individually for initial assessments so that rapport can be established with individuals and they have the opportunity to assert their own problems, their particular perspective of the situation and any interpersonal difficulties within the family situation. The interactive nature of many problems in the family context is acknowledged, and will be further assessed as the intervention progresses.

### The relatives

Six broad assessment themes should be covered during the initial interviewing since these will be critical to the intervention components:

1. Distress in relatives and situations (including thoughts) that trigger distress.
2. Coping strategies used to deal with both positive and negative symptoms, and what effect these have on family members and the patient.
3. The relative's understanding about the illness, the symptoms, medication and so on.
4. The consequences of the illness on the relative, including any restrictions (e.g. to social life, occupation) and financial hardship.
5. The relationship with the patient and the identification of dissatisfactions the relative has about particular aspects of his or her behaviour.
6. Areas of strength: for example an effective coping strategy, social supports, positive relationship with the patient.

The Camberwell Family Interview (CFI) (see Leff and Vaughn, 1985) provides an excellent format for assessing these areas. Since many practitioners may not have access to this instrument some of its important content areas are listed in Table 3.2.

Following the content areas outlined in the table, the interview should establish the chronological history of the patient's illness from the viewpoint of the relative. A time period of the last three months can be used to focus on current problems or symptoms that the relative perceives the patient to be experiencing in the home or community environment. Some details of the nature, frequency and context of such difficulties should be established, the relative's behaviour and feelings in response to the problems, the reactions of other family members, and so on. A more detailed analysis of the behaviours can be made in later stages of the assessment and intervention. The initial interview aims to establish the broad areas of difficulty and to develop rapport with the relative by facilitating them in giving an overview of events and their reactions. Attention should be paid to the assessment of communication problems between family members, and particularly the frequency of expressions of

Table 3.2   Content areas for relative assessment interview

1. *Background information*
Who lives in the household? (their age, sex, relationship to patient, employment) any recent changes in the household composition?
The contact time of the relative and other household members with the patient

2. *Psychiatric history of the patient*
Obtain a chronological account of the history of the illness, beginning "when did you first notice something different about .....'s behaviour"
For all problems or symptoms mentioned ask about onset, severity, context, reactions and effects on the relative and other household members
Note hospital admissions and the reactions of the relative to these

3. *Current problems/symptoms*
Has the patient experienced problems with sleep/appetite/bodily complaints/under or overactivity/slowness/withdrawal/fears–anxiety/worry/depression/self-care/delusions/hallucinations/odd behaviour/finances/drugs or alcohol?
The nature, severity, frequency of the problems and relatives' reactions and coping responses as well as those of other family members should be ascertained

4. *Relationships between family members*
Irritability/tension or quarrelling from or between members of the household (including the patient) should be assessed

5. *General information about the relative*
Social, occupational activities and interests of the relative; relationship with the patient and other household members; how relationships and activities and interests have been affected by the illness

irritability or the occurrence of disagreements or arguments in the household. It is a good idea to emphasise that irritability and arguing are normal within families and particularly in the context of mental illness, to make relatives feel more at ease with this line of questioning. For example, when discussing the presence of irritability in the patient, the CFI introduces this with: "one of the ways in which this kind of trouble affects people is to make them more snappy, or more likely to fly off the handle at things that would't normally worry them ...". After establishing any irritability of the patient, examples of how this occurs and with which family members should be sought, as well as any examples of arguments or disputes between other family members. The latter might be introduced by suggesting that most people in families disagree or argue from time to time.

The interview may take an hour and a half or longer to complete, since it is often the first time that the relative has been encouraged to talk at length about their experiences. More than one meeting may be necessary for this. It is useful to audiotape the session(s), with the relative's permission, so that its content may be understood and summarised in terms of the relatives's difficulties, strengths and their areas of need (see below).

Other assessments which are useful following from the interview include:

1. A measure of psychological distress in the relative, for example the General Health Questionnaire (GHQ) (Goldberg, 1972) or the Symptom Rating Test (Kellner and Sheffield, 1973).
2. The Family Questionnaire (FQ) (Barrowclough and Tarrier, 1987: Tarrier and Barrowclough, 1987). This is a checklist of patient focused problems. Forty-nine problems are described with one open "other" category to allow for any idiosyncratic difficulties. The relative is requested to indicate, on three 5-point scales, the frequency with which the behaviours occur, the amount of distress the behaviours cause them, and how well they feel able to cope with the difficulty.

Following the interview and the administration of other assessments, it is useful to summarise the relative's situation in terms of their problems, needs and strengths. An example is given in Table 3.3.

Such a constructional approach (Goldiamond, 1974) to difficulties should not be seen as a simple restatement of problems: translating problems into needs shifts the emphasis of the assessment away from family deficits and focuses on directions for positive change. The intervention does not seek to eradicate problems but rather to help formulate and meet the needs of the family using and acknowledging whatever resources they have available. Although problems and needs are categorised in Table 3.3, it is apparent that there is a lot of overlap between categories. For example, sources of distress are also coping difficulties and may arise from lack of

Table 3.3 An example of problems, needs and strengths of a relative (mother) summarised from interview, GHQ and FQ assessments

| Problems | Needs |
| --- | --- |
| *Distress* Reports of anxiety with specific situations (e.g. patient drinking excessively and not complying with medication); general worries concerning future of her son; and disagreement with husband about how to react to son's inactivity leading to distress of the mother | Alternative ways of coping with situations that trigger anxiety; further assessment of nature of worries; help with communication and problem solving of difficulties with her husband and son |
| *Coping Strategies* Difficulty dealing with the son staying in bed during the day, and how to react to delusional self-talk (as well as situations above) | Problem-solving and advice on coping strategies |
| *Knowledge about illness* Feelings of guilt about contributing to the illness cause, belief that delusions are controllable by son, worries that medication is addictive | Information about the illness and its treatment |
| *Restrictions to own life style* Little contact with friends due to attending to son's problems and embarrassment about his condition and behaviour; holidays and social life with husband much reduced | To re-establish pleasurable social activities |
| *Dissatisfactions with patient behaviour* Annoyed by son's inactivity and lack of attention to personal hygiene | Assistance with helping son to change behaviours, or in coping with the negative symptoms |
| *Strengths* Keen to work with family programme, support from husband and daughter, several friends who live locally, positive relationship with son, evidence of successful coping with some problems in past, has maintained and enjoyed a part time job | |

understanding about the illness. The function of the summary is to clarify areas of need and to feed these back to the relative; and to indicate the directions of assistance that the intervention might take: success in one aspect of intervention may well facilitate change in another area or meet more than one of the relative's needs.

## The patient

If possible, the patient should be interviewed and similar content areas discussed as used with the relatives. In this way, a chronological account of the illness might be obtained from the patient; their report of past and particularly current symptomatology sought and how it has affected or continues to affect everyday activities; details of how the illness has affected his/her life generally; and the nature of any problems in the family or community contexts discussed. In practice, long interviews and detailed questioning of the patient may be impossible, particularly when the patient is acutely ill or actively psychotic. As with the relatives, the aim of the assessment is to identify problems and strengths so that areas of need may be ascertained.

Three broad areas of assessment are important, and it is advisable to use some form of assessment scales to obtain information about them.

1. *Symptomatology.* The Psychiatric Assessment Scale (PAS) (Krawiecka, Goldberg and Vaughan, 1977) is useful for assessing current symptomatology. The reports of other members of the interdisciplinary team should be sought, as well as relatives' assessments and the patient's own report. Past symptomatology may be examined from these reports and careful reading of hospital case notes.
2. *Social functioning.* The Social Assessment Scale (SAS) (Birchwood et al., 1990) is recommended. This may be completed using the relative(s) as informant.
3. *Patient strengths.* This assessment should include the interests of the patient (especially including past interests since often the patient has few current activities or interests); skills and areas of competency; social supports and friends (including positive contacts with agencies such as day care).

## The interventions

The interventions may be divided into three components: education about the illness, stress management including coping strategies, and goal setting for patient behaviour change. It should be emphasised that:

1. These components should not be seen as discrete or time limited: for example, giving relatives information about schizophrenia does not end when the education component has been "delivered" to the relatives.
2. The aim of the interventions is to address the needs of the family and accordingly, with each family some components or intervention aspects

will be much more important than others: for example, where relatives are experiencing very high levels of distress and/or where the patient is severely handicapped by unremitting psychotic symptoms, it may be more appropriate to concentrate on helping the relative to manage their distress and to cope with difficult patient behaviours than to set goals aimed at directly changing patient behaviour.

3. Assessment is an integral part of treatment, and each intervention begins with a detailed analysis which takes as a starting point the information collected in the initial assessments with the patient and relatives.

4. At all times, it is important to communicate assessments and interventions with members of the multidisciplinary team who are involved with the patient's treatment.

## Education

Beginning the interventions with education about schizophrenia has several useful functions, not least of which is to help "engage" the family members in treatment. Many relatives have been told very little about the illness and most regard access to detailed information about schizophrenia as a need of high priority. The education sessions also serve to present the theoretical framework or rationale in which other work with the family will take place. This rationale emphasises that schizophrenia is a stress-related, biological illness influenced in its course by the social environment: the family members are in no way to blame for having caused the illness, but on the contrary are an important resource in assisting in the patient's recovery.

### Assessment prior to giving information

1. In accordance with the collaborative approach to intervention which we have advocated, an understanding of the relatives' beliefs and attitudes about the illness in general and the symptoms of the patient in particular is a necessary precondition to establishing an interactive mode of information presentation rather than delivering a lecture about schizophrenia. If they have not already received much information, it is likely that they will have formulated some ideas of their own, and if they have had some education about the illness they may still have misconceptions and areas of ignorance. Information from the initial interviews will be useful, and it is advisable to collect more detailed information using for example, the Knowledge about Schizophrenia Interview (KASI) (Barrowclough et al., 1987). The KASI aims to assess the relative's

information, beliefs and attitudes about six broad aspects of the illness:
*Diagnosis*—what kind of problem does the relative think the patient is being treated for?
*Symptomatology*—does the relative believe the "key" symptoms (such as the relative themself has identified) are part, of the illness or personality related? Is the relative aware of florid symptoms? Do they understand that negative symptoms are features of the illness?
*Aetiology*—what caused the illness according to the relative?
*Medication*—is the relative aware of the long term and prophylactic nature of the medication?
*Prognosis*—does the relative accept the possibility of recurrence and what does he/she think might cause relapse?
*Management*—what does the relative think he/she should or shouldn't do to assist the patient's recovery?

2. It is also advisable to have a detailed knowledge of the patient's past and present psychopathology: the content of their delusions, nature of hallucinations, behaviours related to these symptoms (e.g. belief that the TV is broadcasting their thoughts is associated with refusal to enter TV room or smashing of TV set), negative symptoms, and variation in symptoms across episodes of acute illness. Is the patient aware of the diagnosis? Do they accept that they have a mental illness? Do they have any objections to disclosing details of their symptoms to their wife, mother, father or other relatives?

A useful format for giving the information component when there is more than one key relative is to assess the relatives' existing level of knowledge in short individual sessions and to present information to them collectively. There are no hard and fast rules as to when and how to include the patient in the sessions: factors such as the age of the patient, their relationship to the relative and their current level of functioning may influence such decisions. A parallel but separate information-giving session for the patient is often useful, with their joint attendance at the end of the relatives' session or at a later session with the rest of the family. In the first instance allowing the relatives to see the therapist without the patient present may be preferable: there are often questions the relative wants to raise which they would feel uncomfortable talking about if the patient were there. For example, will she ever work again? will he ever recover? as well as issues of guilt or embarrassment about the problems. One of the benefits of having the patient attend the later discussion of the illness with the relatives can be their communication of feelings and thoughts experienced during the illness. The relatives only see behavioural correlates of florid symptoms and may be unaware of the thinking and fears behind seemingly impulsive and bizarre behaviours. However not all patients will be able to or will wish to communicate their "experiential" symptoms.

The education component of the intervention may involve two or more initial sessions. The first would consist of a brief assessment followed by presentation and discussion of information paying particular attention to misunderstandings about the illness that the relative holds. Details of aspects of the condition that the relative simply does not know can be given. Discussion should be prompted referring frequently to the relatives' beliefs about the condition (for example, "when we were talking earlier you mentioned that you felt that Peter stayed in bed too much and you wondered whether this was due to his medication or because he was lazy. Another explanation could be the illness itself. Some of the symptoms of the illness are called negative symptoms. These symptoms include difficulty in doing ordinary things, and it is quite common that people want to sleep or to lie around more than usual.") Acceptance of the relative's viewpoint while suggesting alternative explanations is the starting point of changing the relatives' beliefs and engaging them in a more positive approach to the management of patient difficulties. Care should be taken not to overload the relative with too much information or with medical jargon. The aim is to help the relatives acquire information likely to have a beneficial influence on their interactions with the patient rather than to learn academic or technical knowledge.

It is useful to see relatives and patients together for the latter part of the session, and if appropriate the patient is encouraged to describe the thinking which directed his or her actions during periods of acute illness and disturbed behaviour. A short interval between the first education session and follow up is advisable during which time the family is asked to read an information booklet covering the material presented in the session. Relatives occasionally become worried or misunderstand information. An early second appointment provides an opportunity for discussion of such difficulties.

At the second appointment relatives and patient may be seen together, and further discussion prompted. The therapist should actively encourage the relatives to consider any problems they have in assimilating explanations about the illness and its treatment which differ from those previously held. For example, "when we talked earlier, you said that you were worried that your daughter might get addicted to the medication and would be better off without it. What do you think about that now?" A post test of knowledge following this session is useful in assessing areas where further attitude or belief change will be important, since it is unlikely that relatives, particularly those where patients have a long history of illness, will change all their views after a brief educational component.

## Stress management and coping responses

This component of the intervention focuses primarily on the needs of the relatives and aims to reduce their levels of reported distress using cognitive behavioural approaches. The decision whether or not to include the patient for all or part of the sessions depends as always on the needs of the family. A flexible approach is the most useful, allowing relatives some time to discuss assessment of stressors without the patient present when the patient may be seen in a parallel session, but bringing the family together to assess situations or to plan change strategies that involve interactions between members.

The component should be introduced with a clear rationale. Some relatives may misguidedly think that they are to blame for the illness or are not coping as well as they might, so care should be taken to not to strengthen these ideas. The rationale might emphasise the following points:

1. Living with a person who suffers from schizophrenia can be very difficult, and most relatives feel stressed and upset, at least some of the time.
2. When the patient returns to live with the family, a lot of the day-to-day help and rehabilitation is carried out by family members. Hence it is important to make sure that they have help in managing their stress and coping with difficult situations if they are to effectively help the patient.
3. Additionally, people who suffer from schizophrenia are unusually sensitive to stress in others, so by feeling more in control oneself, you may indirectly help the patient.

*Assessment*

As with all cognitive behavioural interventions, a detailed assessment of agreed problems with feedback to the relatives encouraging active participation in finding ways to control and thus reduce stressful situations is the format of the intervention. Hence assessment should be seen as an integral part of treatment. A simple explanation of the tripartite analysis of stress—thoughts, feelings and behaviour—is given, following which relatives are encouraged to give examples of situations which have triggered stress responses in the previous week. Examples from the initial interview or other assessment source may be suggested by the therapist. For example from Table 3.3, the relative would be encouraged to describe thoughts, feelings and behaviours associated with the situations given under "distress" and "coping strategies" headings. The relatives would then be given practice in recording the situations and their responses, and asked to complete individual records of instances which occur during the interval before the next session. These records are then used at subsequent sessions to build up descriptive behavioural analyses of the antecedents and consequences (cognitive, behavioural, physical) of problem situations at home; and the analyses are fed back to the relatives whose collaboration is sought in finding more effective ways of coping with the situations.

### Example 1

A mother lives alone with her son, John, a man in his late thirties who has an 18-year history of schizophrenia with unremitting delusions of persecution. John received a monthly depot injection at the local health centre. Each month the day before it was due he would typically announce to his mother that he was going to phone the centre, refuse to have the injection and tell the staff what he thought of them, that is, verbally abuse them and accuse them of plotting against him to make him ill. His mother became extremely distressed and tense, wondering what she would do if he missed the injection and became more ill and was concerned that he would swear at and abuse the centre staff. She felt responsible for John's behaviour: "What will they think of me, letting him phone?" was a predominant thought. She would attempt to reason with John not to phone, an argument would ensue, with John swearing and shouting at his mother. The situation would continue throughout the day, with John threatening to phone and his mother repeatedly attempting to dissuade him. Eventually he would phone and abuse the staff.

Further details of the situation were elicited at interview. "When did you first begin to feel stressed?" The mother reported that she picked up "signs" that John was going to be difficult some time before the problem began, and she would feel physically tense and anticipate difficulties. "What happened when John made the phone call?" It emerged that the staff would usually persuade John to come in for his injection, which he did if not the next day then some days later. Alternative strategies to cope with the situation were explored, including the mother telling John she thought it was important to get his injection, but to phone the centre if he wanted to speak to the staff about it. The consequences of such a strategy were discussed, and the mother's thoughts were challenged, e.g. "the staff will think I'm terrible for letting him speak like that, causing them all that trouble", "If I don't try and persuade him he may not get his medication". The alternative response was role played with the therapist, and work was done helping the mother to calm her anticipatory anxiety with positive self statements when she expected the situation to arise. When the mother felt confident to do so, the strategies were implemented, reviewed and modified, and further difficult situations were then targeted.

### Example 2

Andrew was in his mid-twenties, had a three-year history of schizophrenia and lived with his parents. He would frequently leave the bathroom in an untidy state. The father reported that this made him very annoyed. He would think "He's lazy, ill or not, he should be able to hang his clothes up". He would tell his wife who felt that the untidy bathroom was a trivial matter, and since it was she who cleaned the house, did not understand why her husband was annoyed. She felt that her husband was not concerned enough with Andrew's problems and that he did not understand the illness. Andrew's father felt that his wife was "too soft" on the son.

Further analysis of the situation determined that it was usual that the situation was discussed in the mornings when both parents were rushing out to work. It was agreed that they should discuss their attitudes to the son's behaviour more fully at a more appropriate time and reach a consensus agreement. They decided to include Andrew in the discussion about the bathroom, and he agreed to attempt to be tidier, i.e. not leave his clothes and the wet towel on the floor. The therapist discussed the negative symptoms of schizophrenia and the importance of using prompts to initiate behaviours. The use of prompts was rehearsed with the parents in this particular situation, and the assumptions of the father about using prompts were challenged, e.g. "I shouldn't have to remind him to do ordinary things" and of the mother about her husband's behaviour, e.g. "getting annoyed about Andrew and the bathroom means that he doesn't care about his son's real problems".

The approach outlined for intervening to reduce stress in relatives emphasises the following points:

1. A detailed analysis of situations associated with stress is essential, including the interactive nature for other family members. The use of role play may facilitate assessment.
2. It is important to look for predictability in situations. Much stress in relatives is cumulative resulting from difficulties accruing over time. Feelings of irritability, tension or arguments are more understandable and controllable if the pattern of their escalation is highlighted.
3. Patient-focused behaviour may often be the trigger for feelings of stress, but the perceived or actual reactions of other people, especially members of the family, may be the most important factors in increasing and maintaining stress.
4. The use of role play to rehearse alternative strategies is important for their effective implementation. Cognitive factors, for example beliefs about the illness which conflict with proposed strategies or dysfunctional assumptions about the behaviour of others, may interfere with implementation and should be dealt with in the sessions.

## Goal setting

One of the principal aims of the intervention is to improve the social functioning of the patient. Using the format of goal planning and seeing the whole family together, the aim is to teach the family a constructional approach to the problems of family members. This entails seeing problems as needs which might be best met through promoting positive behaviour change.

### Assessment

The chief assessment tool is a strengths/needs list which is completed about the patient, but which may include the needs of other family members. This tabulates on the one hand the patient's abilities, interests and resources and on the other hand difficulties, issues or problems. Family members (including the patient) are asked to complete this individually, and the patient is encouraged to include items pertaining to his relatives. The lists are then pooled and information from earlier assessments, for example initial interviews or questionnaires are used by the therapist to identify further issues of concern. It is often necessary to probe for patient strengths, for example what were the patient's interests before the illness? Are the family overlooking patient abilities as too ordinary to mention, but which may be important for future plans, for example the ability to drive or a particular work skill? An example of a strengths/needs list is given in Table 3.4.

*Intervention*

1. The needs of the family are reviewed and rank ordered by the family in terms of priority and being realistic to achieve in the short term. It is important that the needs are seen as important to the patient, or are linked to other needs which have higher priority for him or her. For example, doing the housework may have priority for the relatives, whereas the patient may only be concerned with getting his or her own accommodation in the case of a parental household. The patient may see that improving say cooking skills would be an advantage and a step

Table 3.4   Example of a strengths/needs list and goal plan for a teenage girl living with her parents

| Strengths | Problems/Issues areas for change | Needs |
|---|---|---|
| *Interests* music, clothes, reading, tennis, seeing friends, watching "soaps" on TV, *Abilities* 'O' levels and good academic record at school, typing, driving licence, cooking skills, good listener and enjoys helping others *Resources* parents, sister and several friends and relatives keen to help; school helpful to assist her return | *parents won't leave me alone in house *worry about missing school *feeling tired & lethargic *overweight spends a lot of time in bed, doing very little when up, avoiding friends and relatives, not interested in personal appearance | 1. Parents to discuss and plan to go out without daughter 2. Return to school 3. Review tiredness 4. Reduce weight 5. Get back to reasonable getting up/bedtimes 6. Engage in more activities 7. Get back to seeing friends/relatives 8. Take more interest in personal appearance |

* problems identified by the patient

towards independent living whereas cutting the grass may hold no interest or incentive.

2. After identifying the need, the strengths list is scanned for approaches that might be used to meet the need.
3. A goal is then set and stated in clear behavioural terms and where necessary it is broken down into small quickly attainable steps.
4. The relatives' and patient's participation in the goal step is reviewed be this an active, facilitating, or passive role—the latter being desirable if the relative's response is intrusive or fosters dependency.
5. At the next session progress with the goal step may be reviewed, efforts reinforced, goals changed, abandoned or new steps commenced.

In using goal setting with schizophrenic patients it is important to incorporate prompts into the execution of plans and also to maximise the reinforcing value of achieving goal steps: a common difficulty for patients is in initiating behaviour and the patient may feel that the effort required to perform a task may not be equal to the subjective value of the goal. Hence the importance of beginning with small steps which achieve goals of importance to the client. Any failure to achieve the goals should be viewed as a planning failure, since one otherwise risks reducing the low self efficacy of the patient and further diminishing their "motivation", and possibly in making the relatives feel that the patient "is not trying".

## SOME CONCLUDING COMMENTS

The above guidelines are intended for working with individual families. We know rather less about the efficacy of working with groups of relatives, and there do seem to be problems of maintaining relatives' attendance at group meetings. Even with individually planned sessions, many of the reviewed studies have families who decline help or who quickly drop out, and where patients in these families have been followed up, they appear to have a poor prognosis (Smith and Birchwood, 1990). A commitment to working with the family over an extended time period is important, with a nine months to a year time frame of weekly/fortnightly then monthly appointments, followed by less frequent but regular contact. Engaging the family in interventions may be more difficult in cases of longstanding illness, where relatives have had little previous support, and have become alienated from services. A collaboration between relatives, patients and practitioners is required to extend the optimism of research findings into clinical practice.

# REFERENCES

Barrowclough, C. and Tarrier, N. (1984) Psychosocial interventions with families and their effects on the course of schizophrenia: a review. *Psychological Medicine*, **14**, 629–42.

Barrowclough, C. and Tarrier, N. (1987) A behavioural family intervention with a schizophrenic patient: a case study. *Behavioural Psychotherapy*, **15**, 252–71.

Barrowclough, C. and Tarrier, N. (1990) Social functioning in schizophrenic patients. I: The effects of expressed emotion and family intervention. *Social Psychiatry and Psychiatric Epidemiology*, **25**, 125–9.

Barrowclough, C., Tarrier, N., Watts, S., Vaughn, C., Bamrah, J.S. and Freeman, H. (1987) Assessing the functional value of relatives' reported knowledge about schizophrenia. *British Journal of Psychiatry*, **151**, 1–8.

Birchwood, M. and Smith, J. (1987) Schizophrenia and the family. In: Orford, J. (ed.), *Coping with Disorder in the Family*, Lawrence Erlbaum, London.

Birchwood, M., Smith, J., Cochrane, R., Wetton, S. and Copestake, S. (1990) The social functioning scale: the development and validation of a scale of social adjustment for use in family intervention programmes with schizophrenic patients. *British Journal of Psychiatry*, **157**, 853–9.

Cardin, V.A., McGill, C.W. and Falloon, I.R.H. (1986) An economic analysis: costs, benefits and effectiveness. In: Falloon, I.R.H. (ed.), *Family Management of Schizophrenia*, John Hopkins University Press, Baltimore.

Cheek, F.E., Laucius, J., Mahnoke, M. and Beck, R. (1971) A behavior modification training programme for parents of convalescent schizophrenics. In: Rubin, R. (ed.), *Advances in Behaviour Therapy*, Vol. 3, Academic Press, New York.

Creer, C. and Wing, J.K. (1974) *Schizophrenia in the Home*, National Schizophrenia Fellowship, Surbiton.

Dawson, M.E., Liberman, R.P. and Mintz, L.I. (1989) Sociophysiology of expressed emotion in the course of schizophrenia. In: Barchoz, P. (ed.), *Sociophysiology of Social Relationships*, Oxford University Press, New York.

Ehlert, U. (1989) Psychosocial intervention for relatives of schizophrenic patients. In: Emmelkamp, P., Everaed, W., Kraaimaat, F. and van Son, M. (eds), *Advances In Theory and Practice in Behaviour Therapy*, Swets & Zeitlinger, Amsterdam.

Fadden, G., Kuipers, I. and Bebbington, P. (1987) The burden of care: the impact of functional psychiatric illness on the patient's family. *British Journal of Psychiatry*, **150**, 285–92.

Falloon, I.R.H. and Pederson, J. (1985) Family management in the prevention of morbidity of schizophrenia: the adjustment of the family unit. *British Journal of Psychiatry*, **147**, 156–63.

Falloon, I.R.H., Boyd, J.L., McGill, C.W., Razani, J., Moss, H.B. and Gilderman, A.M. (1982) Family management in the prevention of exacerbations of schizophrenia. *New England Journal of Medicine*, **306**, 1437–40.

Falloon, I.R.H., Boyd, J.L. and McGill, C. (1984) *Family Care of Schizophrenia*, Guilford Press, New York.

Falloon, I.R.H., Boyd, J.L., McGill, C.W., Williamson, M., Razani, J., Moss, H.B., Gilderman, A.M. and Simson, G.M. (1985) Family management in the prevention of morbidity of schizophrenia: clinical outcome of a two year longitudinal study. *Archives of General Psychiatry*, **42**, 887–96.

Goldberg, D. (1972) *The Detection of Psychiatric Illness by Questionnaire*, Maudsley Monographs No. 21, Oxford University Press, London.

Goldiamond, I. (1974) Towards a constructional approach to social problems:

ethical and constitutional issues raised by applied behaviour analysis. *Behaviourism*, **2**, 1–84.

Goldstein, M.J., Rodnick, E.H., Evans, J.R., May, P.R. and Steinberg, M.R. (1978) Drug and family therapy in the aftercare of acute schizophrenia. *Archives of General Psychiatry*, **35**, 1169–77.

Hatfield, A.B. (1987) The expressed emotion theory: why families object. *Hospital and Community Psychiatry*, **38**, 341.

Hogarty, G., Goldberg, S., Schooler, N.R., Ulrich, R.F. and EPICS Collaborative Study Group (1974a) Drug and sociotherapy in the aftercare of schizophrenic patients. II: Two year relapse rates. *Archives of General Psychiatry*, **31**, 603–8.

Hogarty, G., Goldberg, S., Schooler, N.R. and EPICS Collaborative Study Group (1974b) Drug and sociotherapy in the aftercare of schizophrenic patients. III: Adjustment of non-relapsed patients. *Archives of General Psychiatry*, **31**, 609–18.

Hogarty, G., Schooler, N.R., Ulrich, R.F., Mussare, F., Ferro, P. and Herron, E. (1979) Fluphenazine and social therapy in the aftercare of schizophrenic patients. *Archives of General Psychiatry*, **36**, 1283–94.

Hogarty, G., Anderson, C.M., Reiss, D.J., Kornblith, S.J., Greenwald, D.P., Javan, C.D. and Madonia, M.J. (1986) Family psychoeducation, social skills training and maintenance chemotherapy in the aftercare treatment of schizophrenia. 1: One-year effects of a controlled study on relapse and expressed emotion. *Archives of General Psychiatry*, **43**, 633–42.

Hogarty, G., Anderson, C.M. and Reiss, D.J. (1987) Family psychoeducation, social skills training and medication in schizophrenia: the long and the short of it. *Psychopharmacological Bulletin*, **23**, 12–13.

Hudson, B. (1975) A behaviour modification project with chronic schizophrenics in the community. *Behaviour Research and Therapy*, **13**, 339–41.

Kellner, R. and Sheffield, B.F. (1973) A self-rating scale of distress. *Psychological Medicine*, **3**, 101–6.

Kottgen, C., Sonnichsen, I., Mollenhauer, K. and Jurth, R. (1984) Results of the Hamburg Camberwell family Interview study, I–III. *International Journal of Family Psychiatry*, **5**, 61–94.

Krawiecka, M., Goldberg, D. and Vaughan, M. (1977) A standardised psychiatric assessment scale for rating chronic psychotic patients. *Acta Psychiatrica Scandinavica*, **55**, 299–308.

Leff, J. and Vaughn, C. (1985). *Expressed Emotion in Families: Its Significance for Mental Illness*, Guilford Press, New York.

Leff, J., Kuipers, L., Berkowitz, R., Eberlein-Fries, R. and Sturgeon, D. (1982) A controlled trial of intervention in the families of schizophrenic families. *British Journal of Psychiatry*, **141**, 121–34.

Leff, J., Kuipers, L., Berkowitz, R. and Sturgeon, D. (1985) A controlled trial of social intervention in the families of schizophrenic patients: Two year follow-up. *British Journal of Psychiatry*, **146**, 594–600.

Leff, J., Berkowitz, R., Shavit, A., Strachan, A., Glass, I. and Vaughn, C. (1989) A trial of family therapy v. a relatives group for schizophrenia. *British Journal of Psychiatry*, **154**, 58–66.

Leff, J., Berkowitz, R., Shavit, A., Strachan, A., Glass, I. and Vaughn, C. (1990) A trial of family therapy v. a relatives group for schizophrenia: Two-year follow-up. *British Journal of Psychiatry*, **157**, 571–7.

Lefley, H.P. (1989) Family burden and family stigma in major mental illness. *American Psychologist*, **44**, 556–60.

Reynolds, I. and Hoult, J. (1984) The relatives of the mentally ill: a comparative trial of community-oriented and hospital-oriented psychiatric care. *Journal of Nervous and Mental Disease*, **172**, 480–9.

Smith, J. and Birchwood, M. (1990) Relatives and patients as partners in the management of schizophrenia: the development of a service model. *British Journal of Psychiatry*, **156**, 654–60.

Tarrier, N. (1989) Electrodermal activity, expressed emotion and outcome in schizophrenia. *British Journal of Psychiatry*, **155** (Suppl. 5), 51–6.

Tarrier, N. and Barrowclough, C. (1987) A longitudinal psychophysiological assessment of a schizophrenic patient in relation to the expressed emotion of his relatives. *Behavioural Psychotherapy*, **15**, 45–57.

Tarrier, N., Barrowclough, C., Vaughn, C., Bamrah, J.S., Porceddu, K., Watts, S. and Freeman, H. (1988) The community management of schizophrenia: a controlled trial of a behavioural intervention with families to reduce relapse. *British Journal of Psychiatry*, **153**, 532–42.

Tarrier, N., Barrowclough, C., Vaughn, C., Bamrah, J.S., Porceddu, K., Watts, S. and Freeman, H. (1989) The community management of schizophrenia: a two year follow-up of a behavioural intervention with families. *British Journal of Psychiatry*, **154**, 625–8.

Tarrier, N., Lowson, K. and Barrowclough. C. (1991) Some aspects of family interventions in schizophrenia. II: Financial considerations. *British Journal of Psychiatry*, **159**, 481–4.

Terkelsen, K. G. (1983) Schizophrenia and the family: II. Adverse effects of family therapy. *Family Process*, **22**, 191–200.

Test, M.A. and Stein, L.I. (1980) Alternatives to mental hospital treatment. *Archives of General Psychiatry*, **37**, 409–12.

Turpin, G., Tarrier, N. and Sturgeon, D. (1988) Social psychophysiology and the study of biopsychosocial models of schizophrenia. In, Wagner, H. (ed.), *Social Psychophysiology: Perspectives on Theory and Clinical Application*, John Wiley, Chichester.

Vaughan, K., Doyle, M., McConaghy, N., Blaszczynski, A., Fox, A. and Tarrier, N. (in press (a)) The Sydney intervention trial: a controlled trial of relatives' counselling to reduce schizophrenic relapse. *Social Psychiatry and Psychiatric Epidemiology*.

Vaughan, K., Doyle, M., McConaghy, N., Blaszczynski, A., Fox, A. and Tarrier, N. (in press (b)) The relationship between relatives' expressed emotion and schizophrenic relapse: An Australian replication. *Social Psychiatry and Psychiatric Epidemiology*.

Vaughn, C. (1986a) Comments on Dulz and Hand. In: M.J. Goldstein, I. Hand and K. Hahlweg (eds), *Treatment of Schizophrenia: Family Assessment and Intervention*, Springer-Verlag, Berlin.

Vaughn, C. (1986b) Patterns of emotional response in the families of schizophrenic patients. In: M. J., Goldstein, I. Hand and K. Hahlweg (eds), *Treatment of Schizophrenia: Family Assessment and Intervention*, Springer-Verlag, Berlin.

# Chapter 4

# Early Intervention

MAX BIRCHWOOD, FIONA MACMILLAN AND JO SMITH

INTRODUCTION

Early intervention in schizophrenia is a much-discussed ideal with an appealing simplicity, yet its conceptual and practical underpinnings remain limited. *When* early intervention should take place, *what* it should seek to change and *how* it should do so, are crucial issues which can barely be answered at the moment.

This chapter will concentrate on a limited but nevertheless important component of early intervention: namely, the availability of strategies to prevent or abort an impending episode of acute schizophrenia. Emphasis is laid upon co-operation of psychological and medical approaches, describing in detail the theoretical background and practical intervention strategies which are presently being developed.

The prevention or amelioration of relapse is important for the future well-being of the individual with schizophrenia. It is known that each relapse brings with it an increased probability of future relapse, residual symptoms and accompanying social disability (World Health Organisation, 1979). Even an ideal combination of pharmacological and psycho-social intervention does not ablate the potential for relapse (Hogarty et al., 1986). Studies of first episode patients suggest that early intervention before or during the first episode may have a disproportionate impact on future vulnerability to relapse compared to future episodes. The Northwick Park study (Macmillan et al., 1986) followed up 253 first episode patients over 2 years, of which 120 took part in a placebo-controlled trial of maintenance neuroleptic medication. The period of time between the individual's loss of well-being and presentation to services and time in treatment combined ("duration of untreated illness") was carefully documented; they found that the shorter the duration of untreated illness, the less likely the patient was to relapse over the following 2 years. Duration of untreated illness is to some degree associated with insidious onset which predicts a poor outcome; but in many cases relates to serendipitous factors determining the promptness of access to care. The clear implication is that the more quickly schizophrenia is recognised and intervention initiated, the greater the chances of survival become. Reducing this apparently critical period is no easy task, since there are known to be a number of filters that operate between the first experience of distress or disorder and presentation to specialist services (Goldberg and Huxley, 1980). Ian Falloon and colleagues in the rural area of Buckingham in the UK, are attempting to meet this problem by training GPs in the early recognition of (first episode) schizophrenia, thus prompting rapid medical and psychosocial intervention. The Buckingham project represents an innovative approach to early intervention which is presently being evaluated and whose outcome could have profound implications for service provision.

Other efforts have therefore concentrated on the less ambitious goal of early intervention to abort an impending relapse in individuals with an existing history of vulnerability to schizophrenia. Although such individuals may be well known to services, clinicians may have only modest ability to anticipate the potential for relapse. In a small study of 14 patients, Pyke and Seeman (1981) demonstrated the practical difficulty in predicting the potential for relapse when they exposed patients on maintenance therapy to a 6-week period free of drug treatment, repeated at 6-monthly intervals, aimed to reduce or discontinue the maintenance therapy. The cohort was drawn from ordinary clinical practice, including some individuals with tardive dyskinesia, some who were well and symptom-free, and a small group with residual symptoms who insisted on participation against the judgement of the clinicians. Eight patients suffered recurrences, four of whom required inpatient treatment. One patient who had been symptom-free and well for 11 years on small doses of oral neuroleptic suffered an acute relapse 3 months after discontinuation, another who participated against the advice of clinicians, remained well and symptom-free for two and a half years following discontinuation.

Studies of very large groups exposed to dose manipulations of neuroleptic therapy (Kane, Woerner and Sarantakos, 1986) suggest that the response of individuals is difficult to predict. Kane suggests that elucidation of subgroups is necessary to determine those individuals who may remain well on minimal doses. This is extremely difficult in clinical practice and may confound routine use of low-dose strategies.

Although clinicians may be only modest predictors of relapse potential in individuals, this does not prevent early recognition of loss of well-being, nor preclude early intervention. McCandless-Glincher et al. (1986) studied 62 individuals attending for maintenance therapy, and enquired about their recognition of and response to reduced well-being. The patients were drawn from those routinely attending two medical centres; their age range (20–75 years) with a mean illness duration of 28 years, suggests that such a group would be well represented in ordinary clinical practice. Sixty-one said they could recognise reduced well-being; of these thirteen relied upon others to identify symptoms for them. Nine were assisted by others and thirty-six identified the problem themselves. The majority (fifty out of sixty-one) of patients initiated some change in their behaviour when they recognised reduced well-being, including engaging in diversionary activities, seeking professional help and resuming or increasing their neuroleptic medication. Only three of this group had ever been encouraged to self-monitor by mental health professionals, and a further seven had received encouragement from relatives. Thus these schizophrenic patients had initiated symptom-monitoring and a range of responses almost entirely at their own initiative.

In essence, there may be a relatively untapped pool of information which is not being accessed adequately enough to initiate early intervention, except perhaps by patients themselves. If individuals can recognise and act on symptoms suggestive of reduced well-being, then it is possible that patterns of prodromal episodes heralding relapse may be apparent and identifiable. Studies of prodromes of relapse have been conducted in research centres which lend support to this possibility which we now review.

## STUDIES OF PRODROMES

### Clinical studies

While reports of clinical studies lack observational rigour and objectivity they have provided important insights into the phenomenology of decompensation. The most common approach is the detailed case study that retrospectively gathers information after a relapse, from the patient and family members (e.g. Chapman, 1966). Past reviewers of the early literature (Donlan and Blacker, 1975; Docherty et al., 1978) distinguished four sequential stages of relapse. Although the clinical literature is not sufficiently powerful to clearly support the validity of these stages and their suggested sequential relationship, they provide a useful framework for descriptive purposes.

The first stage, described by many authors, is a feeling of loss of control over cognitive and perceptual processes. McGhie and Chapman (1961), Bowers (1968) and Freedman and Chapman (1973) describe cases where the individual is initially aware of heightened mental efficiency, creativity and general well-being. Birchwood et al. (1989) described a patient who abruptly discontinued medication due to a sensation of well-being, only to relapse; and a further two cases who experienced a similar feeling of well-being prior to the onset of decompensation. However, this "euphoria" quickly subsides as the individual begins to experience a diminution of control over cognitive–perceptual processes. This is described in most of the clinical reports as a feeling of over-stimulation, involving a difficulty in preventing internal or external events invading consciousness (e.g. Chapman, 1966). Visual, proprioceptive and time distortions are common resulting in visual illusions and feelings of derealisation and depersonalisation "… irrelevant thoughts and feelings appear from nowhere and cannot be separated from more meaningful ones … the patient becomes a passive recipient … past memories and present occurrences, varying in length, relevance and emotional tone that run through his mind, leaving him fearful and perplexed" (Donlan and Blacker, 1975, p. 324). Perhaps not surprisingly it has been reported that patients will consult their physicians with vague, diffuse symptoms which are suggested to be the result of activated biological systems (Offenkrantz, 1962).

The onset of depressive-like symptoms is widely reported in the second stage and is regarded by some as a psychological reaction to deteriorating mental processes. These include low mood, lowered self-esteem, vegetative signs and social withdrawal (Cameron, 1938; Stein, 1967; Donlan and Blacker, 1975). Chapman's (1966) classic study notes an absorbing self-concern and preoccupation with aberrant mental functions and experiences. The uncertainty this creates may be responsible for obsessional rituals which Chapman notes as characteristic of the prodrome in some of his patients. Those with prior experience of relapse may feel a sense of foreboding; this, in the context of intact insight, may be the trigger for self-administration of medication observed by Brier and Strauss (1983) and McCandless-Glincher et al. (1986). Such changes were clearly associated with impairment of role performance.

Some authors describe a further third stage characterised by impulsivity, exaggeration of normal emotions and an inability to exercise control over the expression of personal thoughts. "She began atypically to lose her temper and spend money freely … she bought an automobile and drove it impulsively without a licence … (she acted) in a rebellious urge to obtain what she wanted for her life" (Docherty et al., 1978). The disinhibition tends to be progressively more primitive, including sexuality, rage, demands for attention and concerns about death ["I'm not afraid of anyone anymore, I hate everyone, I hate good, I'm going to burn the world" (Donlan and Blacker, 1975)].

Many of the cases described in the clinical studies suggest a fourth stage which includes experiences of ''pre-psychotic'' thinking: these include delusional mood, ideas of reference, a sense that one's thoughts have an alien quality and losing trust in people. Perceptual misinterpretations are frequently reported and delusional-like explanations may be entertained to make sense of these experiences.

The clinical studies do not reveal a homogeneous picture of prodromes of schizophrenia partly because they are based on observations of over 30 patients taken in different epochs by clinicians schooled in different psychiatric traditions. There is some consensus in observation of pre-psychotic changes (anxiety/agitation and dysphoria) but less agreement in respect of other "borderline" symptoms (disinhibition and "pre-psychotic" thinking). However, it is possible that the transition to full relapse may be as variable *between* subjects as the characteristics of an episode itself. The strong emphasis on phenomenology in these studies has shown that early signs of relapse are inappropriately caricatured as "neurotic" symptoms— i.e. in terms of Foulds' (1976) notion of a hierarchy of psychiatric illness, according to which schizophrenia, at the top of the hierarchy, will concurrently incorporate dysphoria, anxiety and other neurotic symptoms. The loss of control over normal mental processes is widely observed and probably plays a significant role in the genesis of "neurotic" symptoms giving them a unique character. In fact, in the retrospective study by Hirsch and Jolley (1989 see below), "fear of going crazy" was the most prevalent early symptom reported by 70% of their relapsing patients.

The clinical studies have offered a set of hypotheses for further examination. They have not provided information about the duration of prodromes, the validity of the "stages", their sequential relationship, nor the survival of insight. All of these aspects are prerequisites for clinical application.

### Retrospective studies

The interview study by Herz and Melville (1980) in the USA attempted systematically to collect data from patients and relatives about early signs of relapse. It is widely regarded as definitive since they interviewed 145 schizophrenic sufferers (46 following a recent episode) as well as 80 of their family members. The main question, "could you tell that there were any changes in your thoughts, feelings or behaviours that might have led you to believe you were becoming sick and might have to go into hospital?", was answered affirmatively by 70% of patients and 93% of families. The overall agreement between patients and families was 66%. The study did not, however, determine the reasons for the discrepancy between patients and family members.

Generally the symptoms most frequently mentioned by patients and family members were dysphoric in nature: eating less (53%), trouble concentrating (70%), troubled sleep (69%), depression (76%) and seeing friends less (50%) . The most common "early psychotic" symptoms were hearing voices ( 60% ), talking in a nonsensical way (76%), increased religious thinking (48%) and thinking someone else was controlling them (39%).

A similar British study (Birchwood et al., 1989) interviewed relatives of 42 CATEGO "S" schizophrenic patients recently admitted or discharged from inpatient care. All relatives recalled "early signs" but 19% could not specify when they occurred. Table 4.1 summarises results of this study together with parallel data from Herz and Melville (1980). There is considerable agreement in the content of the early signs although somewhat less in their relative frequency. Both studies concur in finding "dysphoric" symptoms the most commonly prevalent. In the Herz and Melville study although more families than patients reported the presence of early signs, there was considerable concordance between patients and families in the content and relative significance of early symptoms. There was substantial agreement between patients that non-psychotic symptoms such as anxiety, tension and insomnia were part of the prodrome but less agreement as to the characteristics of the earliest changes. Fifty per cent of the patients felt

Table 4.1   Percentage of relatives reporting early signs

| Category | Birchwood et al. (1989) (n = 42) | | Herz and Melville (1980) (n = 80) | |
|---|---|---|---|---|
| | % | Rank* | % | Rank* |
| Anxiety/agitation | | | | |
| Irritable/quick tempered | 62 | 2(eq) | — | — |
| Sleep problems | 67 | 1 | 69 | 7 |
| Tense, afraid, anxious | 62 | 2(eq) | 83 | 1 |
| Depression/withdrawal | | | | |
| Quiet, withdrawn | 60 | 4 | 50 | 18 |
| Depressed, low | 57 | 5 | 76 | 3 |
| Poor appetite | 48 | 9 | 53 | 17 |
| Disinhibition | | | | |
| Aggression | 50 | 7(eq) | 79 | 2 |
| Restless | 55 | 6 | 40 | 20 |
| Stubborn | 36 | 10(eq) | — | — |
| Incipient psychosis | | | | |
| Behaves as if hallucinated | 50 | 7(eq) | 60 | 10 |
| Being laughed at or talked about | 36 | 10(eq) | 14 | 53.8 |
| "Odd behaviour" | 36 | 10(eq) | — | — |

* There were many other symptoms assessed. Percentage reporting only shown for parallel data.

that the characteristic symptoms of the prodrome were repeated at each relapse. A number of these patients also reported that many of the non-psychotic symptoms persisted between episodes of illness, an important issue to which we shall return below.

Both studies carefully questioned respondents about the timing of the onset of the prodrome. Most of the patients (52%) and their families (68%) in the Herz and Melville study felt that it took more than a week between the onset of the prodrome and a full relapse. Only 10% of patients and families believed that the time period was less than a day. Similarly, Birchwood et al. (1989) found that 59% observed the onset of the prodrome one month or more prior to relapse, and 75% two weeks or more. Nineteen per cent were however unable to specify a time scale.

These studies systematise relatives' and patients' experiences of the prodromal period, finding the characteristic symptoms to be predominantly non-psychotic, and of sufficient duration to enable the implementation of an early intervention strategy. Such a strategy would require the compliance of the patient, which might not always be forthcoming without sustained insight. Heinrichs et al. (1985) examined the survival of insight retrospectively in a group of 38 DSM-III schizophrenics who had relapsed. A systematic retrospective case note analysis indicated that insight was present in 63% of relapses, a figure confirmed by an independent interview with the responsible clinicians. They also found that retention of insight predicted a much better response to early intervention. In those with early insight, 92% responded well to rapid intervention, as compared to only 50% without early insight.

## Prospective studies

The true predictive significance of prodromal signs can only be clearly established with prospective investigations. Such studies need to examine three issues: (a) Whether prodromes of psychotic relapse exist; (b) to what extent there are similarities and differences to those identified in the clinical and retrospective studies, and (c) how often the "prodromes" fail as well as succeed to predict relapse (i.e. "sensitivity" and "specificity"). The clinical implications of this research will largely depend on the degree of specificity which early signs information affords. In particular a high false positive rate will tend to undermine the use of an early intervention strategy that uses raised doses of neuroleptic medication since in such cases, patients will have been needlessly exposed to additional medication.

The first prospective study of prodromal signs was reported by Marder et al. (1984a). In the course of a study comparing low and standard dose maintenance medication, patients were assessed on a range of psychiatric symptoms at baseline, 2 weeks later, monthly for 3 months and then every 3 months. Relapse was defined as the failure of an increase in medication to manage symptoms following a minor exacerbation of psychosis/ paranoia ratings. Thus under this definition it is not known how many genuine prodromes were *aborted* with medication and whether those that responded to medication were similar to those that did not. Of the 41 DSM-III chronic schizophrenic men who took part in the study, 14 relapsed. Patients were assessed using a standard psychiatric interview scale (BPRS—Overall and Graham, 1962) and a self-report measure of psychiatric symptoms (SCL-90: Derogatis et al., 1973). Changes in scores "just prior to relapse" were compared with the average ("spontaneous") change for a given scale during the course of the follow up period. Marder et al. (1984a) found increases in BPRS depression, thought disturbance and paranoia and SCL-90 scores for interpersonal sensitivity, anxiety, depression and paranoid ideation prior to relapse. Marder et al. note that the changes they observed were very small (equalling 2 points on a 21-point range) and probably not recognisable by most clinicians. A discriminant function analysis found the most discriminating ratings were paranoia and depression (BPRS) and psychotism (SCL-90). They suggest "such a formula if used in a clinic could probably predict most relapses although there would be a considerable number of ... false positives" (p. 46). While this study strongly supports the presence of the relapse prodrome, and some of the characteristics described by Herz and Melville (1980), it was unable to control for timing. The last assessment before relapse varied from between 1 and 12 weeks, weakening the observed effects. One would anticipate the prodrome to be at its maximum in the week or two prior to relapse; assessments carried out prior to this would measure an earlier and weaker stage of the prodrome, or miss it entirely.

Subotnik and Nuechterlein (1988) considerably improved upon the Marder study by administering the BPRS bi-weekly to 50 young recent onset schizophrenic patients diagnosed by RDC criteria. Twenty-three patients relapsed and their BPRS scores 2, 4 and 6 weeks prior to the relapse were compared with their scores in another 6-week period not associated with relapse and with scores of a non-relapse group ($N = 27$) over a similar period. This research found that BPRS Anxiety–Depression (which includes depression, guilt and somatic concern) and Thought Disturbance (hallucinations and delusions) were raised prior to relapse. Increases in "odd thought content" were more prominent as relapse approached (2–4 weeks prior to relapse). The contrast with the non-relapsed patients revealed a rise in low-level "psychotic" symptoms as part of the prodrome, but not of the non-psychotic items (depression, somatic concern, guilt, etc.). This suggests that the non-psychotic symptoms are sensitive to relapse but not specific to it. If however, they were followed by low-level psychotic symptoms, then this study suggests that relapse is more probable. It is also possible that elevations in anxiety–depression may be predictive in certain individuals. Subotnik and Nuechterlein note: "... mean elevations in prodromal symptoms were small ... 0.5–1.00 on a 7-point scale ... but in three patients no prodromal symptoms were present ... in several others they did not begin to show any symptomatic change until 2–4 weeks prior to relapse ... thus lowering the magnitude of the means" (p. 411). These results support clinical observation, that the nature and timing of prodromal signs are like relapse itself—not universal, but including considerable between-subject varia-bility. Nevertheless Subotnik and Neuchterlein reported that a dis-criminant function using two BPRS "psychotic" scales correctly classified 59% of relapses and 74% of non-relapse periods, suggesting a false positive rate of 26%.

Hirsch and Jolley (1989) in the course of an early intervention study measured putative prodromes ("neurotic or dysphoric episodes") in a group of 54 DSM-III schizophrenics using the SCL-90 and Herz's Early Signs Questionnaire (ESQ; Herz, Szymonski and Simon, 1982). Patients and their key workers received a one-hour teaching session about schizo-phrenia, particularly concerning the significance of the "dysphoric" syn-drome as a prodrome for relapse. This enabled them to recognise "dysphoric episodes", a task made more feasible as all subjects were symptom-free at the onset of the trial. At each dysphoric episode, the SCL-90 and the ESQ were administered and then weekly for two further weeks; otherwise each was rated monthly. Relapse was defined as the re-emergence of florid symptoms including delusions and hallucinations. Seventy-three per cent of the relapses were preceded by a prodromal period of dysphoric and neurotic symptoms within a month of relapse. These prodromes were defined clinically but confirmed by SCL-90 scores which were similar to those reported by the other two prospective studies and included depression, anxiety, interpersonal sensitivity and paranoid symptoms. Interpretation of this study is complicated by the design in which half the subjects received active and half placebo maintenance medi-cation and all patients showing signs of dysphoric (prodromal) episodes were given additional active medication (Haloperidol, 10 mg per day). Dysphoric episodes were much more common in the placebo (76%) than in the active group (27%) but the prompt pharmacological intervention does not allow us to ascertain whether these dysphoric episodes were part of a reactivation of psychosis (i.e. true prodromes) aborted by medication and to what extent these included "false positives" related, perhaps, to the use of placebo.

This study confirms the existence of a prodromal period of approximately 4 weeks duration characterised by non-psychotic symptoms including:

(a) mild depression or dysphoria, anxiety and interpersonal sensitivity; and
(b) low-level psychotic symptoms including suspiciousness, ideas of reference and a feeling that the individual does not "fit in" with others around him.

One interesting result of the study arose from the administration of the ESQ interview questionnaire designed by Herz and Melville and reproduced in Table 4.2. This shows the importance of symptoms of dysphoria/depression and general blunting of drives and interests and highlights the phenomenological experience of psychotic decompensation, which are not generally part of the psychopathology examined by BPRS and SCL-90. Experiences such as "increased perceptual intensity", "puzzlement about objective experience", "racing thoughts" and "loss of control" and "fear of being alone" capture the phenomenological schemas which were described so lucidly in the clinical studies.

A further prospective study conducted by the authors (Birchwood et al., 1989) involved the development of a scale designed to tap the specific characteristics of the prodrome rather than that of general psychopathology. Construction of the scale was informed by the previous retrospective study reported and underwent extensive psychometric validation. Birchwood et al. (1989) developed scales to be completed by both the patient and an observer (e.g. relative, carer, hostel worker). There were four concerns (relating to the clinical application of early signs monitoring) that influenced this development. First the identification of early signs by a clinician would require intensive, regular monitoring of mental state at least bi-weekly which is rarely possible in clinical practice. Second, some patients choose to conceal their symptoms as relapse approaches and insight declines (Heinrichs and Carpenter, 1985). Third, many patients experience persisting symptoms, cognitive deficits or drug side-effects which will obscure the visibility of the prodromes. Indeed the nature of a prodrome in patients with residual symptoms (in contrast to those who are symptom-free) has not been studied and is important since in clinical practice the presence of residual symptoms is the norm. Fourth, the possibility is raised that the characteristics of prodromes might vary from individual to individual and that this information may be lost in scales of general psychopathology and group designs in research studies.

The authors developed an ongoing system of measurement, where patients and observers completed the scale fortnightly; at out-patient clinic attendance, with a community psychiatric nurse or through the mail.

Table 4.2 Frequency of emergent symptoms during prodromal episodes (Herz Early Signs Questionnaire). Reproduced from Hirsch and Jolley (1989)

| Emergent symptom | Prodromal episodes (n = 44) (%) |
|---|---|
| Fear of going crazy | 70 |
| Loss of interest<br>Discouragement about future | 60–70 |
| Labile mood<br>Reduced attention and concentration<br>Preoccupation with one or two things | 50–60 |
| Feelings of not fitting in<br>Fear of future adversity<br>Overwhelmed by demands<br>Loss of interest in dress/appearance<br>Reduced energy<br>Puzzled/confused about experience<br>Loss of control<br>Boredom<br>Thoughts racing<br>Indecisiveness | 40–50 |
| Distanced from friends/family<br>Feeling that others do not understand<br>Disturbing dreams<br>Loneliness | 30–40 |
| Reduced sex drive<br>Fear of being alone<br>Increased energy | 20–30 |
| Increased perceptual intensity<br>Increased sex drive<br>Depersonalisation<br>Religious preoccupation | 10–20 |
| Ideas of reference<br>Elevated mood<br>Risk taking | 0–10 |

These data were then plotted in an ongoing fashion (Figure 4.1). It was reasoned that the behavioural observations by the observers might provide additional information if the individual under-reported or lost insight. *Changes* in baseline levels were readily apparent, which is particularly important if the individual experiences persisting symptoms.

The authors reported the investigation of 19 young schizophrenic patients diagnosed according to the broad CATEGO "S" class. All except

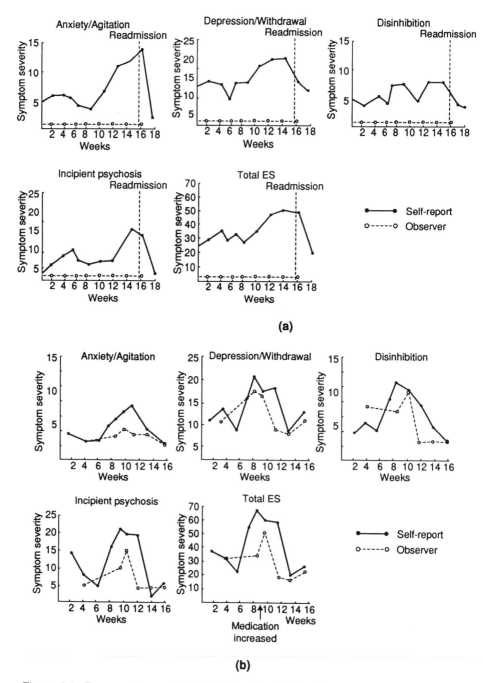

Figure 4.1   Five prodromes detected using the ESS scales.

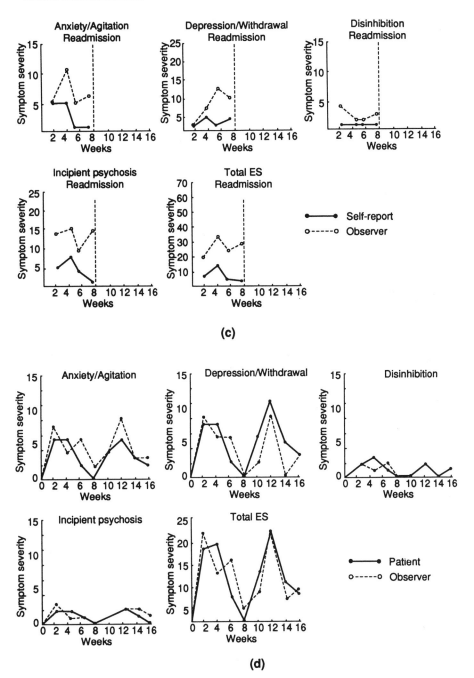

Figure 4.1   (continued).

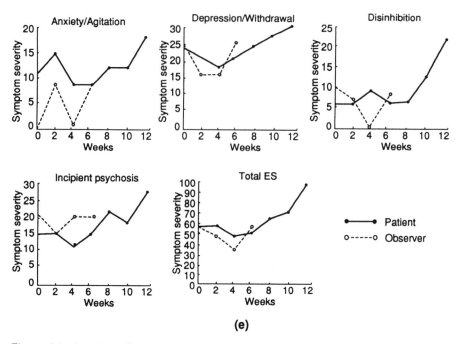

**(e)**

Figure 4.1   (continued).

one were on maintenance medication and monitored in the context of a routine clinical service and were not involved in a drug trial. Eight of the 19 relapsed in the course of 9 months and of these, 50% showed elevations on the scales between 2 and 4 weeks prior to relapse. A *post hoc* defined threshold on their scale (> or <30) led to a sensitivity of 63%, specificity of 82% and an 11% rate of false positives.

This study was a clinical investigation to see how prodrome monitoring might be applied in the clinical setting and to examine in more detail idiopathic aspects of the prodromes. Figure 4.1 show some of the results of individual prodromes. Figure 4.1a is that of a young male who relapsed 16 weeks following discharge. In this case the first change was that of dysphoria/withdrawal which was apparent 5 weeks prior to relapse. After 1–2 weeks he became steadily more agitated and within 2 weeks of relapse, low level ("incipient") psychotic symptoms appeared. Disinhibition was unaffected. In contrast the individual shown in Figure 4.1b reported dysphoria/withdrawal and incipient psychotic symptoms simultaneously together with signs of disinhibition; anxiety/agitation did not peak until somewhat later. It is interesting to note that the observer's behavioural observations showed striking concordance to self-report in respect of dysphoria but lagged behind by up to 2 weeks in respect of the behavioural concomitants of incipient psychosis. These two examples also reveal an apparent *improvement* in well-being just prior to the onset of the prodromes. The third case (Figure 4.1c) is a young male where the rise in anxiety/agitation, dysphoria and incipient psychosis were noted by the observer, but the individual reported a slight rise in symptoms followed immediately by a sharp fall, presumably due to loss of insight. Case four (Figure 4.1d) demonstrates a definite rise in the scales which returned to base line 4 weeks later and was not followed by a relapse. While the scores did not rise above the 30-point threshold, the apparent rise might be regarded as a "false alarm". This particular individual had learnt he had secured employment which seemed to be associated with a feeling of well-being noted by the individual and his mother; as the start of his job approached, his symptoms increased then returned to baseline a few weeks after the start of his job. What was witnessed here was probably the impact of a stressful life event that on this occasion did not culminate in relapse.

The patients in this study were drawn from an outpatient clinic. Many had residual symptoms which were reflected in their baseline scores: Case 1 had moderate negative symptoms and partial delusions; Case 2 also had moderate negative symptoms and heard a "voice" that she knew was part of her illness; Case 3 was asymptomatic. Clinically the detection of a pro-drome in those with residual symptoms is not easily done by reference to absolute scores: comparisons with a baseline are clearly valuable here. The issue is raised as to how *severe* residual symptoms need to be before the concept of "relapse" and therefore of a "prodrome" becomes meaningless. In the cases we have monitored, prodromes have been apparent in those with "mild to moderate" residual positive or negative symptoms but only if some insight continues to be available. In case 5 (Figure 4.1e) a young female continued to hear voices which caused her considerable distress. She had retained some insight but steadily lost it as she found the voice content increasingly plausible. Two weeks prior to this she became more withdrawn and self absorbed and her psychotic symptoms became more generalised.

### Continuing questions

The results of the four prospective studies are consistent with the clinical and retrospective studies, particularly supporting Herz and Melville's (1980) seminal investigation. The studies all found that psychotic relapse was preceded by non-psychotic, "dysphoric" symptoms including anxiety, dysphoria, interpersonal sensitivity/withdrawal and low-level psychotic thinking including ideas of reference and paranoid thoughts. In two of these studies (Marder et al., 1984a; Hirsch and Jolley, 1989) the observations were confounded with a targeted medication strategy, so it was not clear how many of their putative prodromes were actually false positives. It is also possible that the use of an early intervention strategy exaggerated the magnitude of the recorded prodromes. Under normal conditions the baseline levels of psychopathology would be increased in the non-relapsed patients by transient fluctuations in dysphoric symptoms which were not part of a relapse (i.e. the false positives) which might respond to medication, thus reducing the contrast between relapsed and non-relapsed groups.

The possibility of between-subject variability in the nature and timing of prodromes will however act to reduce their apparent amplitude in group studies. Subotnik and Nuechterlein (1988) reported that, some patients showed no prodromal symptoms. Among the patients that did show prodromal signs, some were elevated 6 weeks prior to relapse while in others this occurred a full month later, thus lowering the mean value for the whole group within the time frames (6, 4 or 2 weeks prior to relapse). The study by Birchwood et al. (1989) raises further potential complications as not only does it reveal differences in the amplitude and timing of symptoms, but also that the pattern of prodromal symptoms shows subject variability: some may "peak" on anxiety symptoms, others on disinhibition, and so forth.

The prospective studies have thus raised a number of questions. They have confirmed the existence of prodromes of psychotic relapse, but their limitations have not enabled a clear picture to emerge of the true predicative significance of apparent early warning signs. If the work of Birchwood et al. (1989) is borne out, then group studies in the mould of Subotnik and Nuechterlein (1988) would be inherently limited as they could not capture the apparent qualitative and quantitative differences between patients in their early signs symptoms. This is supported by Subotnik and Nuechterlein's finding that greater prediction came when patients were compared against their own baseline rather than that of other patients. It may be more appropriate to think of each patient's prodrome as a personalised "relapse signature" which includes core or common symptoms together with features unique to each patient. If an individuals relapse signature can be identified, then it might be expected that the overall predictive power of "prodromal" symptoms will be increased. Identifying the unique characteristics of a relapse signature can only be achieved once a relapse has taken place; with each successive relapse further information becomes available to build a more accurate image of the signature. This kind of learning process has been acknowledged by patients (Brier and Strauss, 1983) and could be adapted and developed by professionals and carers as well.

An issue not directly examined in the prospective studies concerns the existence of a prodrome of relapse where the individual continues to experience significant residual symptoms. Where the patient experiences continued negative symptoms such as anergia, alogia and withdrawal, a prodrome presumably will involve an apparent *exacerbation* of these symptoms as shown in some of the cases in Figure 4.1. Where individuals continue to suffer from symptoms such as delusions and hallucinations, a "relapse" will involve an exacerbation of these symptoms; whether these relapses will also be preceded by prodromes of a similar character is unknown. Patients in the Hirsch and Jolley (1989) and Subotnik and Nuechterlein (1988) studies were generally symptom free; there was somewhat more variability in residual symptoms than in the Birchwood et al. (1989) and Marder et al. (1984a) studies. In view of the large numbers of patients with even moderate residual symptoms, this issue deserves serious and careful examination.

Patients participating in the prospective studies generally were young (18–35 years) with a relatively brief psychiatric history. Such individuals are more prone to relapse and tend to be recruited at acute admission or because they were thought to be appropriate for low dose or intermittent drug strategies (c.f. Hirsch and Jolley, 1989). The application of this methodology to older, more stable individuals is another important area for further investigation.

## EARLY INTERVENTION STUDIES

In this section we shall review studies which have used neuroleptic drugs as the main vehicle of early intervention. Brier and Strauss (1983) and McCandless-Glincher et al. (1986) presented evidence that individuals believe they not only have ability to recognise early signs of relapse, but also to initiate methods of self-control. This area has received little systematic attention in the literature and should do so; however, as the prodrome phenomena occupies only a brief time window the conditions for psychological research and treatment are not ideal. Nevertheless, this is an avenue which must be pursued (see Birchwood, 1992).

All the drug studies have involved withdrawing patients from maintenance regimes, monitoring clinical state and providing brief pharmacotherapy at the onset of a prodrome. This paradigm has been chosen with the goal of minimising drug exposure, and therefore side-effects, without prejudicing prophylaxis rather than as a means of further controlling relapse. This issue will be returned to at the conclusion of this section.

Herz, Szymonski and Simon (1982) were the first group to use an intermittent approach in an open pilot study of a small sample of patients withdrawn from maintenance therapy. Over a 9-month period, 11% of the sample relapsed which compares favourably with results of relapse on maintenance therapy from other studies. This team are presently engaged in a comparison of patients maintained on active or placebo maintenance medication and given (intermittent) medication at the onset of a prodrome (Herz et al., 1989). On the preliminary data they present, there was no difference between groups in the severity or duration of prodromes, although the placebo group had *more* prodromes. Few hospitalisations had occurred at the time of their preliminary report.

The best controlled study using this paradigm is that of Jolley and Hirsch (1989) and Jolley et al. (1990) in which 54 stabilised, asymptomatic and thus highly-selected patients were randomly assigned to active or placebo maintenance therapy conditions, with both receiving early drug intervention which involved the administration of 5–10 mg daily of Haloperidol. Each patient was given a starter pack of 3 days of oral medication if they were unable to make contact with the research team at the early sign of relapse. Patients received a brief educational session on entry to the study about prodromes and early intervention. Great reliance was placed on patients to recognise the early signs of relapse. Outcome at one year revealed that significantly more patients experienced prodromal symptoms in the intermittent group (76%) than in the control group (27%) which was accompanied by an increased rate of relapse in the intermittent group (30% versus 7%). However, the groups did not differ in readmission, use of compulsory detention or total duration of hospital stay, suggesting that severe relapse was not affected and was indeed low in both groups. Extrapyramidal side effects were reduced in frequency and severity, particularly akathisia, parkinsonism, sedation and gait. Tardive dyskinesia increased from 32% to 55% in the control group and reduced slightly in the intermittent group (29% to 24%). As anticipated by some observers of the first report (e.g. Harrison, 1989) results at 2 years were at variance with the first year and largely disappointing: relapse was more frequent (50% versus 12%) and more severe in the intermittent group. Total exposure to neuroleptics was reduced by 60% in the intermittent group reflected in a much reduced severity of extrapyramidal side effects, but with no impact on social functioning. During the first year of the study, 73% of relapses were preceded by identified prodromal symptoms; during the second year this fell to 25%. As reliance was placed on patients and families to identify and seek assistance for prodromal symptoms, this suggests "… that the single teaching session at the start of the study does not provide patients and families with an adequate grasp of the intermittent paradigm … ongoing psychoeducational intervention should be an essential component of further studies …" (p. 841).

Carpenter et al. (1990) report the outcome of a study of similar design to Jolley and colleagues in which continuous and intermittent medication regimes were contrasted in a sample of 116 patients randomly assigned to groups but not under double-blind conditions. Thus 57 patients in the targeted group were withdrawn from maintenance therapy and compared to 59 who were not. Both groups received early intervention as in the Jolley study determined by the presence of clinically defined prodromes. Unlike the Jolley study, subjects were not specifically selected as good candidates for drug withdrawal and were engaged in the trial following a period of hospitalisation; thus scores on the BPRS and social functioning scales indicated "... moderate signs and symptoms and moderate impairment of social and occupational functioning" (p. 1144); and in addition the sample were young (mean age 28 years) with a 6-year illness history and only a small number in employment. Results did not support the intermittent regime. Patients experienced a higher rate of hospitalisation (53% vs 36%) and survival analyses indicated that continuous medication was superior throughout the 2 years of the trial. Hospital admissions were however regarded as "brief" in both groups and no other differences were noted between the groups in clinical or social functioning at two years. However, the greater number of hospitalisations in the intermittent group was associated with a lower rate of employment at two years. Drug exposure was lower in the intermittent group but data on side-effects were not reported. Not only was the intermittent regime less effective, but it was also less popular too: 50% refused to continue with the regime (vs. 20% in continuous treatment), presumably due to the higher rate of prodromes and hospitalisation and perhaps patients also found the responsibility placed on them to recognise relapse an excessive one.

In evaluating the results of these studies, a distinction must be drawn between the utility of the paradigm *per se* (i.e. intervention at the onset of a prodrome) and the particular application of this approach in terms of the design and methodology of each study. Experimental designs ask specific questions and hitherto the early intervention studies have asked only whether a targeted regime alone yields comparable prophylaxis to one which combines maintenance *and* targeting with the benefit of minimising side effects. The answer to this is clearly negative. A variant of this design might contrast targeting alone with a maintenance regime alone; this design would have greater clinical validity but raise methodological problems.

Other designs will address different questions. A comparison of continuous with targeted and continuous regimes would inform whether early intervention provides additional prophylaxis to the standard regime. A comparison of "standard" dose maintenance regime with a combined low dose and targeted regime would examine whether the increased risk inherent in this drug reduction manoeuvre can be offset by early intervention. With regard to the first design, the study of Jolley et al. (1990) finds an unusually low rate of relapse over 2 years in the group receiving continuous and targeted regimes (12%) suggesting a possible additive effect. This possibility has yet to be adequately tested. A study by Marder et al. (1984b, 1987) bears upon the second design. In this study patients were assigned to a low (5 mg) or standard (25 mg) dose regime of fluphenazine decanoate every 2 weeks and at the first sign of exacerbation the dose was doubled. If this failed patients were considered to have relapsed, which occurred in 22% taking the lower dose and 20% on the higher dose with fewer side effects in the former. Marder et al. (1984, 1987) found that lower doses carried a greater risk of relapse, but these were not "serious" and were eliminated once the clinician was permitted to double the dose at the onset of a prodrome (the survival curves of the doseage groups were not different under targeted conditions). Although "low" dose strategies do carry an increased risk of relapse, they have yet to be properly tested in the context of a targeted regime and the results of Marder do give cause for optimism. Since it is now widely accepted that maintenance doses in clinical practice may be far higher than necessary and may actually reduce prophylaxis (Teicher and Baldessarini, 1985), a double-blind evaluation of targeting in the context of a lower dose maintenance regime would seem to be the next logical research step.

The methodology used to identify relapse prodromes has relied heavily upon patients' skill and their initiative to alert services. Jolley and Hirsch have suggested that a brief educational session is insufficient for patients to grasp the intermittent paradigm; and the high dropout rate noted by Carpenter, Heinrichs and Hanlan (1987) underlies its unpopularity. This experience suggests that it is unrealistic to expect patients to shoulder this responsibility alone and is best shared with services. It is for this reason that the authors are using a more proactive method of monitoring for prodromes in which the burden of early recognition and intervention is shared (Birchwood, Macmillan and Smith, 1991).

In conclusion, early intervention in the form of targeted (intermittent) regimes are severely cautioned by existing studies. Future studies should pay greater attention to the methodology used to identify prodromes so that the burden is shared with services. The use of the early intervention paradigm in other contexts (e.g. low dose regimes) and specifiable subgroups needs further research. The possibilities are numerous and important and offer the clinician much greater flexibility in clinical management.

## EARLY INTERVENTION PROCEDURES

### Selecting suitable subjects

Individuals with a history of repeated relapse or who are at high risk, for reasons of drug non-compliance, use of a low dose maintenance regime, living alone or in a high EE family environment, may be appropriate. Patients showing severe or early signs of Tardive Dyskinesia may also be considered. Those individuals already in receipt of very high doses of maintenance medication may not be suitable for early intervention based on raised drug dose, since in this context higher doses are likely to meet with diminishing returns. Other procedures for early intervention based on psychosocial measures might be considered in such cases. For those with quite severe drug refractory persisting positive symptoms, discriminating a prodrome against such a background is likely to prove extremely difficult (indeed its very existence is questionable) and early intervention becomes less meaningful in this context. The absence of insight may preclude an individual's acceptance of an early intervention strategy. Indeed the ultimate test will be the individual's acceptance of the approach, which in our experience has much to do with his or her dislike of the dislocation which relapse/readmission can cause, as well as fear of the experience itself. The availability of a close relative or carer to corroborate self-report can maximise information about prodromal signs but must be selected in collaboration with the individual. Further, the kind of early intervention strategy which is to be considered will influence subject selection. An intermittent strategy in the context of withdrawal from maintenance medication will be safe perhaps only in 40% of cases: Jolley and Hirsch (1989) excluded 60% of patients on this basis and Chiles, Sterchi and Hyde (1989) found that only one-third (34.8%) of chronic schizophrenic patients attending a Mental Health Centre were eligible. As discussed earlier, those electing to continue with maintenance medication may still benefit from a targeted strategy involving medication given at the onset of a prodrome. In these cases a low dose maintenance regime might be considered.

### Engagement and education

Early intervention rests on the close co-operation between patient, carer/relative and professionals. In common with many interventions outlined in this book, an ethos of trust and "informed partnership" between these groups must be developed (Smith and Birchwood, 1990). Education about prodromes and early intervention opportunities needs to be provided

Table 4.3   Early signs interview: relatives' version

---

*Stage one*: *Establish date of onset/admission to hospital and behaviour at height of*
        *episode*

"On what date was X admitted to hospital?"
    Prompt: date, day, time; contemporary events to aid recall

"When did you decide X needed help?"
    Prompt: date

"What was X's behaviour like at that time?"
    Prompt: What kind of things was X saying?
            What kind of things was X doing?

*Stage two*: *Establish date when change in X was first noticed*

"So X was admitted to hospital weeks after you decided X needed help ..."

"Think back carefully to the days or weeks before then"

"When did you first notice a change in X's usual behaviour or anything out of the
ordinary?"
    Prompt: Nature, time of change

"Were there any changes before then, even ones which might not seem important?"

*Stage three*: *Establish sequence of changes up to relapse*

"I'd like to establish the changes that took place after that up to (date) when you
decided X needed help"

"What happened next (after last change)?"
    Prompt: Was this a marked change?
            When did this happen?
            Can you give me some examples?
            Repeat question until point of relapse is reached

*Stage four*: *Prompting for items not already elicited*

"During this build up to X's relapse/admission to hospital ..."

"Was X unusually anxious or on edge?"
    Prompt: When did you notice this?
            Prompt items from relevant early signs checklist

"Did X seem low in spirits?"
    Prompt: as above

"Did X seem disinhibited (excitable, restless, aggressive, drinking, etc.)?"
    Prompt: as above.

"Did X seem suspicious or say/do strange things?"
    Prompt: as above.

*Stage five*: *Summary*

"Let me see if I'm clear on what happened before X's admission"

"X was admitted on (date), (number) weeks after you decided X needed help;
X was (describe presentation)"

"You first noticed something was wrong on (date) when X
(describe behaviour) ... then X began to ..."
(Complete description of prodrome)

"Have I missed anything out?"

---

which might be given in the context of general educational intervention about psychosis (Smith and Birchwood, 1985, 1987; Birchwood, Macmillan and Smith, 1991). Education must emphasise that some responsibility is being placed on the individual and relative to recognise a potential relapse and to initiate treatment. Engagement and compliance will be enhanced where the client has a stable, trusting relationship with individuals in the mental health services. As the experience of Jolley et al. (1990) illustrates, this requires psychoeducation to be a continuous feature of this relationship.

## Identifying the relapse prodrome and time window for early intervention

Precise information about the individual's prodrome or "relapse signature" may be obtained through careful interviewing of patient or relative about the changes in thinking and behaviour leading up to a recent episode. This must be fed back to patient and carer and carefully documented by the case manager to enable a more accurate discrimination of any future prodrome.

An interview used by the authors to identify the relapse prodrome is shown in Table 4.3. This involves five stages. The first establishes the date of onset of the episode and the time between this and any admission. The second establishes the date when a change in behaviour was *first* noticed; and in the third and fourth stages the sequence of subsequent changes is established using specific prompts if necessary. Finally, the prodrome is summarised. An example of such a prodrome is shown in Table 4.4.

## Monitoring for prodromes

Predicting (and therefore controlling) an impending relapse is greatly enhanced by closer monitoring of a possible prodrome. In addition, those with residual symptoms, severe drug side-effects or unstable symptoms will benefit from closer observation as the establishment of a baseline will facilitate the discrimination of a prodrome from the background "noise". The prodrome it sketches will also bring greater definition to the "signature", thus providing patient, carer and professional with a learning opportunity to improve prediction on any subsequent relapse.

The items in Table 4.1 have been developed into a series of interval scales by Birchwood et al. (1989) and incorporated into a monitoring system in which patient and observer make fortnightly observations plotted on a graph. The frequency of observation can be increased should there be any cause for concern. Figure 4.1a–d illustrate some data arising from this

Table 4.4  Results of a prodrome interview

| Informant: | Parents |
| Admitted: | 25/5/90 |
| Relapse: | March 1990 (first episode) |
| Change first noted: | October 1989 |

| Early sign | Category | Period prior to relapse (weeks) |
| --- | --- | --- |
| Spending more time alone in bedroom | W | |
| Avoiding contact with family; talking less | W | |
| Stopped interests/hobbies —listening to music and drawing wild life | W | 12–20 |
| Stopped work—"people were picking on him". Accused friends of same | IP | |
| Neglecting personal hygiene—not washing, changing clothes | W | |
| Stood in front of mother naked | D | 8–12 |
| Stealing money from family | D | |
| Irritable and argumentative toward family | D | |
| Accusing family of reading his mind | IP | |
| Said he thought the phone was being interfered with | IP | 4–6 |
| Laughing for no reason | IP | |
| Very preoccupied with TV —sat and stared but not appear to be watching | IP | |

A: Anxiety/agitation   W: Withdrawal/dysphoria   D: Disinhibition   IP: Incipient psychosis.

method. A series of decision rules has been developed and form the basis of an early intervention study presently in progress.

A sense of ownership over these data should be created in the minds of patients and their families so that responsibility for initiating early intervention is a shared one; for example in the author's work, regular updated copies of the graphs are provided for participants. Educating patients and relatives about early signs of relapse, feeding back to them information from the early signs interview, and collaboration in monitoring, should significantly raise the likelihood of early detection and therefore intervention.

### Selecting a targeted dose

The selection of a targeted dose of neuroleptics will depend on many factors; but ultimately the final choice is largely empirical in terms of what is known to be effective for a given patient. In the Jolley and Hirsch (1989) trial, the selected sample of stable, symptom-free patients without maintenance medication received a targeted dose of between 5–10 mg/day of oral Haloperidol for up to 2 weeks. Among a representative *clinical* sample it is difficult to be prescriptive. The dosage of medication effective during a recent relapse can serve as a guide, starting with the minimum dose used and, if necessary, working upwards.

### Crisis counselling

Once a prodrome has been declared, the individual and family need intensive support. The psychological reaction to a loss of well-being, and the possibility that this may herald a relapse, places a significant strain on both parties, which, if unchecked, could accelerate the decompensation process. The availability of support, quick access to the team, the use of stress management and diversionary activities will help to mitigate these effects (Brier and Strauss, 1983). It is possible that a relapse may be triggered by a stressful life event; if so, counselling should be directed towards its resolution. For example, the individual depicted in Figure 4.1e revealed an abrupt change in his early signs record associated with the stress of starting a new job (at week 12 on the graph). (The possibilities for early *psychological* intervention are discussed in Birchwood, 1992.)

## IMPLICATIONS AND CLINICAL APPLICATIONS

The clinical application of early signs monitoring offers considerable opportunity for improving care. However, if the encouraging results of the early intervention studies employing targeted medication are to be realised in clinical practice, careful thought must be given to the identification of individual "relapse signatures", the design of monitoring methodology and the nature of the service response to secure these advances for the well-being of patients.

The relationship between early signs of decompensation and actual psychotic relapse remains unclear. There is unlikely to be a simplistic relationship and evidence suggests that false positives and negatives will occur. We have discussed a number of means to improve the specificity of early signs information using additional information relating to idiosyncratic signs for a given individual.

Experienced staff, engaged in long-term clinics supporting patients often have years of regular contact with a client, and can provide useful information concerning certain key changes which in themselves might go unnoticed, but for a given individual may be highly predictive of relapse. The fuller "relapse signature" that is thus obtained can be incorporated into the early signs monitoring procedure and used as a hypothesis to predict specific idiosyncratic signs which will occur at a subsequent relapse of a given individual. Any additional early signs information observed at this relapse can be added to the signature, thereby increasing the accuracy of prediction with each relapse.

## Monitoring methodology

The strategy of close monitoring by highly trained personnel is impractical in routine care. On the other hand, the use of close monitoring by staff for particular target groups, with a high relapse risk is limited by the ability to reliably select high potential relapse risks. The methodology adopted by Birchwood et al. (1989) harnessing the experiences of patients and their carers in a routine service setting may be possible to apply clinically. This offers the potential for documenting information relating to early signs of relapse for a substantial group of patients, with relatively limited input of professional time. However, it is still probable that a substantial group of patients, who retain very little insight or where loss of insight occurs very early in decompensation, may be unable or unwilling to entertain self-monitoring and are also least likely to consent to observation by another. There are no easy solutions to these problems, although education about the illness may, in some cases, improve insight and key people in the individuals life can be trained to monitor and recognise specific early warning signs and to initiate preventative strategies such as increasing medication, or seeking professional help promptly if relapse is predicted.

Notwithstanding its potential therapeutic value, the notion of self-monitoring does raise a number of concerns about sensitising patients and carers to disability, promoting the observations as critical responses, burdening individuals and carers further with requests for repetitive information at frequent intervals, or increasing the risk of self-harm in an individual who becomes demoralised by an impending relapse. There is no real evidence that self-monitoring is likely to increase the risk of self-harm; indeed, florid and uncontrolled relapse may be more dangerous and more damaging. Engaging patients and carers more actively in the management of the illness may also promote a sense of purposeful activity and have therapeutic benefits *per se*. The repetitive nature of the procedure may be self-defeating in the long term and indeed wasteful in well-stabilised patients. Instituting monitoring at times of stress may be a reasonable alternative to continuous monitoring. Those individuals who develop expertise of monitoring through a number of relapses may develop and sharpen the signature in the minds of professionals and carers alike. Despite the many limitations, if early signs monitoring fulfils even part of its promise, it may for many patients with recurrent episodes, promote learning and lead to increased opportunity for combined efforts to control exacerbations due to stress.

## The service response

For the group of patients who routinely attend clinical appointments, information from monitoring by patients and carers has an identified route of access. If this route were formalised it might be possible to ensure clear responses from the service. However, not all patients attend services and the move away from an institutional model is likely to further devolve care away from centralised services. The difficulty in accessing traditional psychiatric services was well documented by Creer and Wing (1974) and Johnstone et al. (1984), a decade later, describe patchy access to care with particular problems for relocated patients and families. The implementation of case management for the long-term mentally ill may ensure constant service links at a distance, but the utilisation of psychiatric services during critical periods will necessarily require information concerning early signs of relapse to be adequately assessed and harnessed (Shepherd, 1990).

The nature of the service response to information concerning early signs of decompensation is still an open question. Most clinical trials have employed pharmacological interventions upon recognition of early signs of decompensation (Jolley and Hirsch, 1989). Within defined cohorts (as in clinical trials) the use of targeted medication has not been sufficient to cope with individual variation. In the clinical setting, where there is a very wide range of maintenance therapy and where the dose and duration of targeted medication is likely to be vary considerably between individuals, targeted medication would require to be individually tailored. However the implementation of strategies that are already recognised by patients and carers as useful would often be entirely appropriate. Indeed the work of McCandless-Glincher et al. (1986) is particularly encouraging since it suggests that very nearly all patients recognise loss of well-being and the majority institute some change in behaviour at their own initiative in response to this, including engaging in diversionary activities, seeking professional help or resuming and increasing neuroleptic medication. In the face of this information, individuals might be encouraged to employ self-management strategies, e.g. stress management procedures or symptom control strategies (Brier and Strauss, 1983) to initiate preventative actions in terms of increasing the frequency of day-centre attendance, requesting brief admission or enlisting professional support to assist in symptom management. To achieve these ends may require radical service change in the direction of the development of a more responsive and flexible service than currently exists. The resultant service envisaged would need to be proactive rather than reactive and responsive to the needs and concerns of individuals and their carers particularly if these alternative preventative strategies are to be viable.

In summary, routinely monitoring early signs to identify individual relapse signatures opens the possibility for individuals to recognise and act on symptoms suggestive of reduced well being and to initiate early intervention strategies to prevent relapse. However, if the promising results of the research studies are to be systematically applied and incorporated into routine clinical practice a viable system of monitoring needs to be established in order to access information routinely and accurately. The service structure also needs to be adapted in order to facilitate this and to be able to respond flexibly and promptly when relapse is predicted. It is to this end that the authors research efforts are devoted.

## REFERENCES

Berkowitz, R., Shavit, N. and Leff, J. (1990) Educating relatives of schizophrenic patients. *Social Psychiatry and Psychiatric Epidemiology*, **25**, 216–20.
Birchwood, M. (1992) Practice Review. Early intervention in schizophrenia: theoretical background and clinical strategies. *British Journal of Clinical Psychology* (in press).
Birchwood, M., Smith, J., Macmillan, F., Hogg, B., Prasad, R., Harvey C. and Bering S. (1989) Predicting relapse in schizophrenia: the development and implementation of an early signs monitoring system using patients and families as observers. *Psychological Medicine*, **19**, 649–56.
Birchwood, M., Macmillan, F. and Smith, J. (1992) Early signs of relapse in schizophrenia: monitoring methodology. In: D. Kavanagh (ed.), *Schizophrenia: an Interdisciplinary Handbook*, Chapman and Hall, London.
Bowers, M.B. Jr. (1968) Pathogenesis of acute schizophrenic psychosis—an experimental approach. *Archives of General Psychiatry*, **19**, 348–55.

Brier, A. and Strauss, J.S. (1983) Self control in Psychiatric Disorders. *Archives of General Psychiatry*, **40**, 1141–5.

Cameron, D.E. (1938) Early schizophrenia. *American Journal of Psychiatry*, **95**, 567–78.

Carpenter, N.T., Heinrichs, D.W. and Hanlon, T.E. (1987) A comparative trial of pharmacological strategies in schizophrenia. *American Journal of Psychiatry*, **144**, 1466–70.

Carpenter, W.I., Hanlon, T.E., Heinrichs, D.W., Summerfelt, A.T., Kirkpatrick, B., Levine, J. and Buchanan, R.W. (1990) Continuous versus targetted medication in schizophrenic outpatients: outcome results. *American Journal of Psychiatry*, **147**, 1138–48.

Chapman, J. (1966) The early symptoms of schizophrenia. *British Journal of Psychiatry*, **112**, 225–51.

Chiles, J.A., Sterchi, D. and Hyde, T. (1989) Intermittent medication for schizophrenic outpatients: who is eligible? *Schizophrenia Bulletin*, **15**, 117–20.

Creer, C. and Wing, J. (1974) *Schizophrenia at Home*, National Schizophrenia Fellowship, Surbiton, Surrey, UK.

Davis, J.M. (1975) Overview: maintenance therapy in psychiatry: I. Schizophrenia. *American Journal of Psychiatry*, **132**, 1237–45.

Derogatis, L., Lipman, R. and Covi, L. (1973) SCL-90: an outpatient psychiatric rating scale—preliminary report. *Psychopharmacology Bulletin*, **9**, 13–17.

Docherty, J.P., Van Kammen, D.P., Siris, S.G. and Marder, S.R. (1978) Stages of onset of schizophrenic psychosis. *American Journal of Psychiatry*, **135**(4), 420–6.

Donlan, P.T. and Blacker, K.H. (1975) Clinical recognition of early schizophrenic decompensation. *Disorders of the Nervous System*, **36**, 323–30.

Eckman, T.A., Liberman, R.P., Phipps, C. and Blair, K. (1990) Teaching medication management skills to schizophrenic patients. *Journal of Clinical Psychopharmacology*, **10**, 33–8.

Foulds, G.W. (1976) *The Hierarchical Nature of Personal Illness*, Academic Press, London.

Freedman, B. and Chapman, L.J. (1973) Early subjective experience in schizophrenic episodes. *Journal of Abnormal Psychology*, **82**(1), 45–54.

Goldberg, D. and Huxley, P. (1980). *Mental Illness in the Community*, Tavistock, London.

Harrison, G., (1989) Brief intermittent neuroleptic prophylaxis for selected schizophrenic outpatients. *British Journal of Psychiatry*, **155**, 702–6.

Heinrichs, D., Cohen, B. and Carpenter, W. (1985) Early insight and the management of schizophrenic decompensation. *Journal of Nervous and Mental Disease*, **173**, 133–8.

Heinrichs, D.W. and Carpenter, W.T. (1985) Prospective study of prodromal symptoms in schizophrenic relapse. *American Journal of Psychiatry*, **143**(3).

Herz, M.I., Szymonski, H.V. and Simon, J. (1982) Intermittent medication for stable schizophrenic outpatients. *American Journal of Psychiatry*, **139**, 918–22.

Herz, M.I., Glazer, W., Mirza, M., Mostest, M. and Hafez, H. (1989). Treating prodromal episodes to prevent relapse in schizophrenia. *British Journal of Psychiatry* (suppl. 5), 123–7.

Herz, M.I. (1985) Early signs questionnaire (personal communication).

Herz, M. and Melville, C. (1980) Relapse in schizophrenia. *American Journal of Psychiatry*, **137**, 801–12.

Hirsch, S.R. and Jolley, A.G. (1989) The dysphoric syndrome in schizophrenia and its implications for relapse. *British Journal of Psychiatry* (suppl. 5), 46–50.

Hogarty, G.E., Anderson, C.M. and Reiss, D.J. (1986) Family psychoeducation, social skills training and maintenance chemotherapy in the after care treatment of schizophrenia: I. One year effects of a controlled study on relapse and expressed emotion. *Archives of General Psychiatry*, **43**, 633–42.

Jolley, A.G. and Hirsch, S.R. (1989) The Dysphoric Syndrome in schizophrenia and its implications for relapse. *British Journal of Psychiatry*, **155**, 46–50.

Jolley, A.G., Hirsch, S.R., Morrison, G., McRink, A. and Wilson, L. (1990). Trial of brief intermittent neuroleptic prophylaxis for selected schizophrenia outpatients: clinical and social outcome at two years. *British Medical Journal*, **301**, 847–52.

Johnson, D.A.W., Pasteski, G., Ludlow, J.H., Street, K. and Taylor, R.D.W. (1983) The discontinuance of maintenance neuroleptic therapy in chronic schizophrenic patients. *Acta Psychiatrica Scandinavica*, **67**, 339–52.

Johnstone, E.C., Owens, D.G.C., Gold, A., Crow, T. and Macmillan, J.F. (1984) Schizophrenic patients discharged from hospital: a follow up study. *British Journal of Psychiatry*, **145**, 586–95.

Kane, J.M., Woerner, M. and Sarantakos, S. (1986) Depot neuroleptics: a comparative review of standard intermediate and low dose regimes. *Journal of Clinical Psychiatry*, **47**(5), (suppl. May), 30–3.

Marder, S.R., Van Putten, T., Mintz, J., McKenzie, J., Lebell, M., Faltico, G. and May, R.P. (1987). Low and conventional dose maintenance therapy with Fluphenazine Decanoate. *Archives of General Psychiatry*, **44**, 518–21.

Marder, S., Van Putten, T., Mintz, J., Labell, M., McKenzie, J. and Faltico, G. (1984a) Maintenance therapy in schizophrenia: new Findings. In: J. Kane (ed.), *Drug Maintenance Strategies in Schizophrenia*, pp. 31–49, American Psychiatric Press, Washington, D.C.

Marder, S.R., Van Putten, T., Mintz, J., McKenzie, J., Lebell, M., Faltico, G. and May, R.P. (1984b) Costs and benefits of two doses of fluphenazine. *Archives of General Psychiatry*, **41**, 1025–29.

McCandless-Glincher, L., McKnight, S., Hamera, E., Smith, B.L., Peterson, K. and Plumlee, A.A. (1986) Use of symptoms by schizophrenics to monitor and regulate their illness. *Hospital and Community Psychiatry*, **37**, 929–33.

McGhie, A. and Chapman, J. (1961) Disorders of attention and perception in early schizophrenia. *British Journal of Medical Psychology*, **34**, 103–16.

Macmillan, J.F., Crow, T.J., Johnson, A.L. and Johnstone, E.C. (1986) The Northwick Park first episodes of schizophrenia study. *British Journal of Psychiatry*, **148**, 128–33.

Offenkrantz, W.C. (1962) Multiple somatic complaints as a precursor of schizophrenia. *American Journal of Psychiatry*, **119**, 258–9.

Overall, J.E. and Graham, D.R. (1962) The brief psychiatric rating scale. *Psychological Reports*, **10**, 799–812.

Owens, D.G.C. and Johnstone, E.C. (1980) The disabilities of chronic schizophrenia: their nature and factors contributing to their development. *British Journal of Psychiatry*, **136**, 384–95.

Pyke, J. and Seeman, M.D. (1981) 'Neuroleptic Free' intervals in the treatment of schizophrenia. *American Journal of Psychiatry* **138**(12), 1620–1.

Schooler, N.R. (1986) The efficacy of antipsychotic drugs, and family therapies and the maintenance treatment of schizophrenia. *Journal of Clinical Psychopharmacology*, **6**, 115–95.

Shepherd, G., (1990) Case management. *Health Trends*, **22**, 59–61.

Smith, J. and Birchwood, M. (1985) *Understanding Schizophrenia*, West Birmingham Health Authority, Health Promotion Unit.

Smith, J. and Birchwood, M. (1987) Specific and non-specific effects of educational intervention with families living with a schizophrenic relative. *British Journal of Psychiatry*, **150**, 645–52.

Smith, J. and Birchwood, M. (1990) Relatives and patients as partners in the management of schizophrenia. *British Journal of Psychiatry*, **156**, 654–60.

Stein, W. (1967) The sense of becoming psychotic. *British Journal of Psychiatry*, **30**, 262–75.

Subotnik, K.L. and Nuechterlein, K.H. (1988) Prodromal signs and symptoms of schizophrenic relapses. *Journal of Abnormal Psychology*, **97**, 405–12.

Tarrier, N., Barrowclough, C. and Vaughn, C., et al. (1988) The community management of schizophrenia: a controlled trial of behavioural intervention with families to reduce relapse. *British Journal of Psychiatry*, **153**, 532–42.

Teicher, M.H. and Baldessarini, R.J. (1985), Selection of neuroleptic dose. *Archives of General Psychiatry*, **42**, 636–7.

World Health Organisation (1979) *The International Pilot Study of Schizophrenia*, Chichester: Wiley.

Chapter 5

# Management and Modification of Residual Positive Psychotic Symptoms

NICHOLAS TARRIER

## INTRODUCTION

In the 1950s the development of neuroleptic medication resulted in great advances in the management of schizophrenia. The effectiveness of these drugs to reduce the positive symptoms of schizophrenia is well established (Davis, 1975; Davis et al., 1980), however, up to 30% to 40% of schizophrenic patients will relapse on medication (Leff and Wing, 1971; Johnson et al., 1987). Furthermore, a considerable number of patients will continue to experience persistent delusions and hallucinations (Curson et al., 1985, 1988; Harrow and Silverstein, 1977; Silverstein and Harrow, 1978). Thus despite the apparent effectiveness of neuroleptics, psychotic symptoms still persist and exacerbations and relapses occur frequently. These drugs also produce undesirable and unpleasant side-effects in a considerable number of patients who may default or poorly adhere to their medication regimens as a result. Because of these difficulties other methods of controlling psychotic symptoms have been investigated.

An area of psychological input which is beginning to attract attention is the management of individual psychotic symptoms. This approach can be important in two circumstances:

1. when patients continue to experience persistent residual symptoms which are not responding further to medication; and
2. when alternatives to medication are required: this may occur when patients are particularly susceptible to medication side effects, notably tardive dyskinesia or when adherence to medication is poor or non-existent. The literature has mainly focused on the first circumstance.

The aim of this chapter is to review treatment methods which have previously been used in the psychological management of psychotic symptoms and to describe in more detail a treatment programme devised by the
author.

## SYMPTOM MANAGEMENT METHODS

### Assessment issues

Although the assessment of individual psychotic symptoms would seem a
relatively easy task, it is beset with difficulties. Symptom recognition and
measurement have been used principally for the purpose of psychiatric
diagnosis and to a lesser extent for the identification of relapse. There has
been much less interest in the measurement of symptoms *per se*. Multi-
dimensional assessment of hallucinations and delusions is therefore still in
its infancy and the development of such assessment methods describing
the parameters of psychotic symptoms is a priority for future research
endeavours.

### A review of psychological treatments

A number of approaches have been reported that attempt to treat psychotic
symptoms through psychological means. These approaches are reviewed
briefly below.

#### Contingency management

Methods based on the operant tradition of psychology have been used to
manipulate rewards and punishments contingent on specified behaviours.
This method has reached its zenith in institutional settings in the token
economy (e.g. Paul and Lentz, 1977). Contingency management has also
been used to decrease the behavioural correlates of hallucinations and
delusions.

A number of methods have been used including social reinforcement
(Ayllon and Haughton, 1964; Liberman et al., 1973; Bulow, Oei and
Pinkey, 1979), time out (Davis et al., 1976), social interference (Alford and
Turner, 1976; Turner, Herson and Bellack, 1977; Alford, Fleece and
Rothblum, 1982), punishment (Bucher and Fabricatore, 1970; Anderson
and Alpert, 1974; Turner, Herson and Bellack, 1977; Fonagy and Slade,
1982; Belcher, 1988) and negative reinforcement (Fonagy and Slade, 1982).

Although positive results have frequently been reported, there are a number of problems with these approaches:

1. Improvements are rarely long lasting or resistant to extinction.
2. Improvements do not generalise to other settings and situations.
3. While these reports are usually of chronic patients in institutional settings in which some control over contingencies can be maintained, applicability in community settings must be doubtful.
4. The manipulation of contingencies requires overt behaviour to reinforce or punish and in this way overt behavioural correlates of hallucinations and delusions are eliminated or reduced.

Since psychotic symptoms are experiential and largely private mental events, patients may be learning not to talk about their symptoms rather than the symptoms themselves being reduced. Despite these problems and the fact that contingency management alone may have limited general value, especially in the era of community care, operant principles will be an important component of any treatment programme.

*Stimulus control*

A number of case reports have attempted to accurately identify and then modify antecedent conditions to the occurrence of psychotic symptoms. The results are somewhat mixed with some positive (Slade, 1972, 1973; Nydegger, 1972) and some negative results (Slade, 1973; Watts et al., 1973). The approach appears to be dependent on the patient's ability to identify accurately either internal or external antecedents and this may not be possible with all patients. However, it is suggested that this is a promising approach with suitable patients.

*Control of auditory input*

This treatment approach, designed to eliminate auditory hallucinations, involves the manipulation of auditory input and is based on theories which have hypothesised an important relationship between external (physical) stimuli and perception of internal (mental) phenomena (e.g. West, 1962; Horowitz, 1975; Slade, 1976). A number of case studies have reported successful interventions using this approach (Green, Glass and O'Callaghan, 1980; Feder, 1982; Green, Hallett and Hunter, 1983; James, 1983; Birchwood, 1986; Morley, 1987).

*Biofeedback*

Biofeedback has rarely been used with schizophrenic patients, however Schneider and Pope (1982) report on an intriguing use of EEG biofeedback.

They attempted to train nine patients to produce EEG patterns that resembled those associated with neuroleptic-induced clinical improvement. Significance within session changes were observed but there were no session to session changes. Unfortunately no assessments were made of any dimension of psychopathology so the clinical utility of such a procedure cannot be assessed.

### Cognitive modification

*Self-Instructional Training (SIT)*. Meichenbaum and his colleagues produced a treatment programme for schizophrenic patients which involved training the patient in self-instruction in on-task behaviour (Meichenbaum and Cameron, 1973). Initial reports demonstrated improvements in task performance, an increase in "healthy talk" and a decrease in "sick talk" (Meichenbaum and Cameron, 1973; Meyers, Mercatons and Sirota, 1976). Other reports, however, have failed to replicate these findings (Gresen, 1974; Margolis and Shemberg, 1976). In a more recent study Bentall, Higson and Lowe (1987) reported improvements in task performance but these showed poor generalisation to other tasks and there was no evidence of superiority of SIT compared to problem solving training.

*Belief modification*. Cognitive therapy methods which modify patients' beliefs and attitudes have been used very successfully over the last decade to treat a wide range of psychological disorders (e.g. Hawton et al., 1989). The use of cognitive belief modification methods to treat delusional beliefs predates this more widespread use with non-psychotic disorders (Beck, 1952; Watts, Powell and Austin, 1973). Watts and his colleagues in a series of controlled case studies demonstrated that belief modification reduced the severity of the abnormal belief whereas relaxation and systematic desensitisation to social situations (a stimulus control method) did not. Following on from this study a controlled trial of belief modification versus belief confrontation demonstrated the superiority of the former (Milton, Patwa and Hafner, 1978). In some patients confrontation appeared to result in the strengthening of delusional beliefs. Other case studies have also reported positive results for this method (Hole, Rush and Beck, 1979; Hartman and Cashman, 1983; Alford, 1986; Chadwick and Lowe, 1991).

### Modification of cognitive processes

The modification of cognitive processes can be distinguished from cognitive modification as the latter attempts to change conscious and dysfunctional beliefs while the former attempts to address the problems of cognitive and information processing deficits which are assumed to underlie the schizophrenic disorder. A considerable amount has been written on the potential usefulness of modifying basic cognitive processes as a treatment procedure (see Brenner, 1986; Gross, 1986; Magaro, Johnson and Boring, 1986; Spaulding, 1986). However in clinical terms this area is still in its infancy. A number of case studies have reported on multi-element programmes aimed at facilitating cognitive processes (Adams et al., 1981; Spaulding et al., 1986) and Brenner and his colleagues in Bern have reported on a controlled trial of a multi-faceted programme including: cognitive differentiation, social perception, verbal communication, social skills and problem-solving (Brenner et al., 1990). This programme has been shown to be superior to placebo and control groups on a number of tests of cognitive performance and measures of general psychopathology after treatment and at 18 months follow-up. Although the rationale for this approach is plausible, there is still a lack of understanding about cognitive processes and how they relate to schizophrenic symptoms and whether poor cognitive task performance is an index of a basic underlying disorder or a consequence of the schizophrenic illness. Similarly does improvement in task performance with training reflect an improvement in the underlying cognitive deficits or a training effect? Furthermore, do these methods reduce individual hallucinations and delusions and if so what are the mechanisms of change? These questions are unresolved, however, in the light of the considerable research literature on cognitive deficits in schizophrenia this approach is worthy of further investigation.

*Self-management*

A number of studies have utilised a variety of self-management procedures in which patients monitor their experiences, identify them as being illness-related or not, implement a procedure to reduce symptoms when present and reinforce themselves for their successes. Such procedures have been reported to occur naturally in some patients (Breier and Strauss, 1983) and one case report suggested monitoring alone was sufficient to reduce hallucinations (Baskett, 1983). Other approaches which have included elements of self-management have been, use of thought stopping (Erickson, Darnell and Labeck, 1978; Lamontagne, Audet and Elie, 1983) and the self-administration of shock (Weingaertner, 1971). Neither of these methods demonstrated any significant clinical effect. One well-controlled study of an inpatient self-control programme did show a decrease in symptoms, however, these returned to baseline levels once the patient was discharged from hospital (Alford, Fleece and Rothblum, 1982).

*Coping strategies*

A number of studies have examined whether schizophrenic patients who experience persistent psychotic symptoms make any attempt to cope with these symptoms. Coping in this sense refers to cognitive and behavioural efforts to control or master the symptoms or to minimise the distress caused by them. The consistent finding from these studies has been that the majority of patients (range: 67–100%) do use active coping with varying degrees of success (Falloon and Talbot, 1981; Breier and Strauss, 1983; Cohen and Berk, 1985; Tarrier, 1987; Carr, 1988).

These naturalistic studies on the use of coping strategies have suggested that symptoms such as delusions may not be completely impervious to non-pharmacological intervention and systematic training in coping methods could be a productive method of management. This approach clearly has features in common with self-management and also includes other methods such as self-instruction and stimulus control. Three characteristics which tend to distinguish this approach are:

1. There is an attempt to use and build on coping methods already used by the patient. Hence the patient's current coping repertoire is assessed and utilised.
2. Secondly, *in vivo* practice is encouraged: that is during training in coping the patient is encouraged to simulate or even bring on the symptoms and practise the coping strategies and as homework to enter situations in which symptoms usually occur with the aim to practise coping strategies.
3. Lastly, training in coping is not restricted to the application of a single technique but may include an array or combinations of individual coping strategies.

Fowler and Morley (1989) report on five case studies, in which patients were asked to continually monitor their mood states, the frequency of symptoms and three aspects of psychotic experience: the extent to which they could control their symptoms, the extent to which they believed their symptoms to be true and the extent to which they were distressed by their symptoms. One patient showed a marked overall improvement and three others showed improvements on their perceived ability to control their symptoms.

## A SPECIFIC TREATMENT METHOD BASED ON COPING STRATEGIES

The remainder of this chapter will describe a treatment method based on a behavioural analysis of psychotic symptoms and the patient's coping strategies. It involves training and practice in specified coping methods.

## Clinical report

Tarrier et al. (1990) reported case studies of two schizophrenic patients who received what the authors termed Coping Strategy Enhancement (CSE). This involved the careful behavioural analysis of the patient's symptoms including the antecedents and consequences. The patient was first given a detailed rationale of the approach. If the patient lacked insight then the intervention focused on the alleviation to any distress caused by their symptoms. One symptom was targeted and a strategy to cope with it was selected. The strategy was then systematically practised under increasingly more difficult conditions in the treatment session and later as homework. Cognitive strategies were first demonstrated overtly by the therapist, then practised overtly and lastly covertly by the patient. Training in behavioural strategies was through role playing or guided practice. If the strategy was successful another symptom was selected for treatment; if not then the patient was trained in a further coping strategy and so on. The two patients treated in this manner both showed considerable improvements in their symptom. At the six month follow-up one patient had continued to improve while the second had shown some deterioration from his post-treatment level but improvements from the pretreatment were still apparent.

## Evaluation

In an ongoing controlled trial to reduce residual and persistent psychotic symptoms being carried out by the author and his colleagues, CSE is being compared to problem solving (PS)(Tarrier (1987), Note 1). CSE follows the same procedure as described in this chapter. Problem-solving is used as the control treatment using the following procedure. The patient is given the rationale for PS, the procedure is initially practised on a neutral task (e.g. a simple game such as draughts or noughts and crosses) with the therapist firstly modelling the use of overt self-instruction to outline the possible alternative moves and their consequences. A move is then selected and implemented on the basis of the evaluation of the positive and negative consequences of each alternative. This procedure is then practised by the patient overtly and then covertly. A similar procedure is then applied to a standard problem (e.g. how to make new friends). Finally, the patient is asked to apply the PS method to problems that they are experiencing at that time. It will be evident from the descriptions of these two treatments (i.e. CSE and PS) that CSE directly focuses on symptom reduction while PS focuses on broader areas of functioning.

Patients were recruited into the study if they:

1. had had a diagnosis of schizophrenia (including first rank symptoms);
2. they were still experiencing psychotic symptoms which were not responding to medication;
3. they had been ill for at least 6 months;
4. they were living in the community, and
5. were between the ages of 16 and 65.

Patients were randomly allocated to one of two treatment limbs (CSE or PS). Both groups received 10 sessions of the appropriate treatment over a 5-week period. Fifty per cent of subjects in each limb were first entered into a 5-week waiting/no treatment period before treatment started. This allowed the waiting time period to act as a control condition.

In each treatment limb 50% of patients were allocated to high expectancy, in which the positive benefits of the treatment were continually emphasised and the remainder were allocated to neutral expectancy. The manipulation of expectancy of treatment outcome was performed to assess the effect of non-specific factors in the intervention. In a previous study involving the use of applied relaxation training (ART) in the treatment of generalised anxiety, expectations of treatment success were found to be responsible for some of the treatment effect (Tarrier and Main, 1986). Little appears known about the possible effect of such non-specific factors in psychological treatment approaches with schizophrenic patients. Assessment was carried out at pre-waiting period (if appropriate), pretreatment, post-treatment and at 6-month follow-up. The assessment battery included:

1. Psychotic symptoms were elicited using the PSE (Wing, Cooper and Sartorius, 1974) and a number of dimensions were then rated: severity was rated on a 7-point scale (from absent to extremely severe) based on the BPRS scales of unusual thought content or hallucinations (Lukoff, Nuechterlein and Ventura, 1986); conviction of belief, preoccupation with the symptom and interference in functioning caused by the symptom were measured using the method described by Brett-Jones, Garety and Hemsley (1987). At post-treatment and follow-up the PSE was repeated and change scores (Tress et al., 1987) calculated for any psychotic symptom that had been present at pretreatment.
2. Global psychopathology was assessed by use of the Psychiatric Assessment Scale (PAS; Krawiecka, Goldberg and Vaughan, 1977) this rates the following 8 items on a 5-point scale: depression, anxiety, delusions, hallucinations, incoherence of speech, poverty of speech, flat affect and retardation.

3. Social functioning was assessed by means of the Social Functioning Scale (SFS)(Birchwood et al. 1990).
4. Coping strategies were assessed for frequency and efficacy.
5. The problem-solving abilities of the patient were measured on a standardised task.
6. The credibility of the treatment and the patient's expectancy of its success were also assessed after the first session during which the rationale had been given; and the patient's subjective estimate of the benefit of the treatment was assessed at the post-treatment assessment.

At the time of writing 43 patients had been assessed as suitable for the study. Of these nine (21%) had refused to participate. Thirty-four patients had been allocated, fourteen to PS and twenty to CSE. Of these twenty-one had completed treatment, thirteen had completed follow-up and thirteen had completed a waiting/no treatment period. This study is as yet incomplete and any results presented at this stage should be viewed with a certain amount of caution. However, preliminary analyses indicate the following: If the symptom severity score is aggregated across symptoms for each patient then the CSE group show statistically significant improvements over treatment in symptom severity, whereas no significant change is seen in the PS group or over the waiting/no treatment period. Two (22%) patients in the PS limb show a complete remission of symptoms at post-treatment, however, no other patients show a greater than 50% improvement. In the CSE limb seven (58%) patients show an improvement of 50% or more and two (17%) of these show a complete remission of symptoms at post-treatment. Patients in the CSE limb show a decrease in preoccupation, conviction and interference of their symptoms but only the latter reaches significance. Patients receiving PS show a decrease in the strength of conviction of belief in their symptom and preoccupation with their symptoms, only the latter of which reached significance. Both treatment groups show a non-significant decrease in depression and the CSE group show a significant decrease in anxiety. However, neither treatment appears to affect social functioning. There were no changes over the waiting/no-treatment period on any of these measures.

Patients receiving neutral expectancy showed a decrease in symptom severity that just reached significance, while the high expectancy group just failed to reach significance. Hence expectancy does not appear to be an influential factor.

The results at this point indicate a superiority of CSE over PS which in turn is superior to no treatment. We await the completion of the study to see if these improvements are maintained. Research in this area is still at an early stage and there are many important clinical and theoretical questions that need to be addressed. One important direction will be to integrate research on cognitive deficits typically found in schizophrenia and how these relate to the practice of cognitive therapy.

## Clinical procedure

### Assessment

Standardised assessment measures have already been discussed in the section on CSE evaluation. In addition, a thorough assessment of the patients symptomatology and coping skills should be covered through a semi-structured interview.

### Antecedent and coping interview

*The nature of the symptoms.* A thorough knowledge of the patient's current psychopathology is required and each psychotic symptom should be clearly defined. The Present State Examination (Wing, Cooper and Sartorius, 1974) is a suitable instrument for eliciting such symptoms. During the interview each symptom should be elicited and the frequency, the duration, and intensity of each symptom should be ascertained. This information can be obtained by asking general questions such as "how often do you hear the voices talking about you?" and then asking about a specific day, e.g. "how many times did you hear the voices yesterday?" Also the duration of each episode of symptoms should be obtained by asking for how long the voices were heard. This line of questioning will probably elicit a range of time periods and should be followed by questions concerning what would be the usual or typical time period. Similarly the severity of each episode should be asked about through questioning on the loudness of the hallucinations or the strengths of the delusional ideas, how easy or difficult they were to ignore or how preoccupying they were when experienced.

*Elicit the accompanying emotional reactions.* Initially general questions concerning the accompanying emotional reaction should be asked such as "how do you feel when this happens?" and "how does this affect you?" Prompts can also be used such as "do you feel frightened/nervous/angry/fed up/sad, etc?" Once a general emotional reaction to the experience of the psychotic symptom has been elicited, then attempts should be made to obtain more specific examples in terms of somatic sensations, cognition and behaviour. Somatic sensations can be elicited by questioning about how the patient feels physically and prompts can be given concerning specific sensations, for example, "do you experience: your heart beating fast?/your muscles tensing up?/your hands sweating?/butterflies in your stomach?, etc. Similarly, cognitive reactions can be elicited by initially asking general questions such as "what goes through your mind when you feel this way/or hear these voices?" It is important to pick up examples the interviewee may give and use these to make suggestions that elicit further examples. Behavioural reactions can be obtained by asking what the patient does when she/he has their experiences. Questions should then be asked concerning whether these are typical reactions, for example, "do you always feel/think/act like this?", "what else happens?" The interviewer should continue to probe for other alternatives once the first few examples have been elicited. Probe questions should be used to help elicit the patient's account of the emotional consequences of the symptoms and the acceptance of a "yes" response without an account of how the patient felt should be avoided. During this line of questioning, examples and evidence of coping strategies may also be given and these should be noted and used as prompts later in the interview.

*Elicit antecedents.* Questions should now be asked concerning the occurrence of any antecedent or precipitating context for each symptom in turn. Example questions include: "can you tell when (the symptom) is going to occur?", "how do you know?", "when does (the symptom) happen?", "what happens before you experience (the symptom)?" Attempts should be made to elicit: where the person is, what they were doing, who else was there, and so on. Probes should be made to elicit external or environmental stimuli so as to assess regular and consistent antecedents to the symptom. If a number of antecedents are elicited then common elements or characteristics should be ascertained. Once external stimuli have been assessed, then questions should be asked concerning internal stimuli such as physical sensations especially feelings of tension, and cognitive stimuli, e.g. a particular train of thought. When both external and internal antecedents have been elicited possible relationships should be examined, for example do certain internal stimuli always occur in the presence of specific external ones? For example, does the patient frequently feel anxious in social situations which precipitate delusions of reference? Questions concerning apparently obvious antecedents should also be asked, for example, do delusions of receiving messages from the TV only occur when the TV is on. Careful attention should also be paid to whether lack of stimulation (e.g. being alone or inactive) or overstimulation (e.g. being in social situations) act as precipitant. Lastly, it is important to assess how easily the patient can identify antecedents as this may have implications for facilitating treatment.

*Elicit consequences.* In eliciting the consequences of the symptom we are attempting to ascertain the longer-term consequences and not the immediate emotional reactions. That is what the person does in response to the symptoms. Questions should be asked concerning what happens after the symptom has occurred. If the patient repeats their emotional reaction then ask what happens after that or how they deal with their emotions. Here we are looking for examples of the effects of experiencing the symptoms such as social withdrawal and avoidance or reductions and restrictions in the patients behavioural repertoire. These consequences are frequently passive coping attempts which result in behavioural and social difficulties.

*Elicit active coping.* This part of the interview attempts to find out how the patient tries to master the symptoms. As before, initially ask general questions and use this information along with any information obtained earlier in the interview to probe for specific coping strategies. For example, such questions as: "how do you cope with this?", "how do you react to (the symptom)?", "what do you do to make yourself feel better?", "is there anything you can do to get rid of (the symptom)?" are useful probes. Attempt should be made to get the patient to describe their coping in terms of changes in physical sensations, cognitive processes or actions. For example, "is there anything you can do to help yourself by feeling a certain way? (e.g. relaxing)", "how do you do this?" If the patient answers in the affirmative, then follow-up with further probes such as "are there any other ways in which you can relax?" Similarly with cognitive strategies, "can you help yourself by thinking in a certain way or telling yourself certain things?" Care should be taken to ascertain the function of the cognitive strategy: does the patient restrict or narrow the range of items already in attention or is attention switched to another subject? Likewise, behavioural strategies should also be assessed, for example by asking: "can you help yourself by doing something?" Here the actual behaviour should be elicited and the opportunities for its implementation, (e.g. by changing the environment or social context). For example, if the patient indicates that engaging in social interaction is effective then ask about the opportunities to do this. Furthermore, ask about common functions of different strategies, for example, if it appears that social engagement is distracting then ask about other methods of distraction (e.g. "can you distract yourself in other ways?"). Table 5.1 classifies coping strategies.

*Effectiveness of coping.* When a list of coping strategies has been defined, attempt to assess the effectiveness of each. For example, ask "when you (specify the strategy), how much help is this?" Rate each strategy as negligible, moderate or very effective. Strategies that are inconsistently effective should only be rated as negligible or moderate. To be rated as very effective a strategy should be consistently effective and stable across time. The

Table 5.1 Classification of coping strategies

1. Cognitive strategies

(a) Attention Switching
The process of focusing attention on to a stimulus which was not already in attention, e.g. distraction
(b) Attention Narrowing
The process of reducing the range of attention
(c) Self-Statement
The process of using covert verbal behaviour to either direct behaviour or re-attribute the cause of an experience or event.

2. Behavioural strategies

(a) Increased Activity Levels
The action of increasing activities which do not require social interaction, e.g. exercise, walking
(b) Increased Social Activity
The action of initiating social engagement
(c) Decreased Social Activity
The action of disengaging from social interaction or avoiding social interaction. (The short-term use of social engagement may be a useful coping method, however, social avoidance resulting in withdrawal and isolation should be classified as a negative consequence and not encouraged)
(d) Reality Testing
Actions which lead to the testing of various causal explanations of events or their interpretation

3. Sensory strategies
Strategies which involve the modification of sensory input

4. Physiological strategies
Strategies which involve the modification of physiological states. These can be appropriate e.g. relaxation or breathing control, or inappropriate e.g. alcohol or drug abuse.

patient's ability for training in coping should also be assessed, that is, whether she/he uses coping strategies already but inconsistently. If coping results in variable success, elicit under what conditions this variability occurs.

*In conclusion.* Lastly check that (1) the range of symptoms has been completely assessed; (2) where a symptom has been identified, then its occurrence, emotional response, antecedents, consequences and coping responses have been completely assessed. At this point a comprehensive picture of the determinants of the patient's psychotic experience and his/her attempts to deal and cope with them should have been built up. As in cognitive-behaviour therapy an accurate and detailed analysis of the problem and its determinants is essential for successful intervention. The interview also serves the function of building a rapport and relationship with the patient and to demonstrate that you take his or her experience seriously, even if you do have a different explanation of the cause.

*Potential problems.* The probability of the success of this behavioural assessment of psychotic symptoms is increased if the symptoms are discrete, easily identified and viewed as being illness-related. A lack of insight into the nature of the symptoms is less of a problem if the patient recognises the distress these experiences and thoughts can cause even if she/he regards their content as true. The rationale of reducing distress is then frequently acceptable to the patient as a rationale for intervention. Greater difficulty will be encountered if symptoms appear to be diffuse and vague, the patient's accounts of them appear unreliable or varying or when the patient is severely thought disordered or confused. In these cases detailed analysis may prove extremely difficult and more general information may have to be accepted.

### Treatment using coping strategy enhancement (CSE)

The aim of CSE is to systematically teach the patient the use of effective coping strategies to reduce the frequency, intensity and duration of the residual psychotic symptoms and their emotional consequences. The assessment interview should produce detailed and individualised data concerning the patient's symptoms, their maintaining factors and his/her coping. The data should be used as a basis for generating interventions based on knowledge of antecedents and coping.

### Education and rapport building

As with all cognitive behavioural interventions an approach of "collaborative empiricism" should be adopted. To enhance this collaborative endeavour between the therapist and the patient it is advisable to provide the patient with detailed information about schizophrenia and the rationale for this treatment approach. Such information can be obtained from appropriate texts (e.g. Barrowclough et al., 1985; Barrowclough and Tarrier, 1992). It is likely that some patients will reject some or all of this information. The therapist should not dismiss the patient's personal explanation of his or her experience, but rather suggest that they agree to differ at this point with a view to putting the different explanations to experimental test at a later stage. Later, appropriate predictions can be generated from the therapist's illness model and the patient's personal model which should be tested out in reality (see later in the text). At this early stage, however, both parties should agree to focus on reducing the associated stress experienced by the patient.

*Procedure*
1. From the assessment information a target symptom should be selected on the basis of either ease of treatment (i.e. the symptom which has clearly identified and modifiable antecedents, for which the patient has clearly identified or partially successful or appropriate coping strategies) or being of high priority (i.e. causing the patient considerable distress or disruption to functioning).
2. Select an appropriate coping strategy from those that occur naturally or one which seems most appropriate or potentially successful (Table 5.1).
3. Again explain the rationale to the patient and obtain feedback indicating that the patient has understood the rationale.
4. Put the coping strategy into action, where possible using the antecedents to the symptoms as contextual cues.
   (a) Where appropriate systematically practice the coping strategy within the session:
      (i) first practice the strategy in isolation, asking the patient to rate on a 0–10 scale how easy/successful they were with the implementation;
      (ii) generate the symptom or alternatively simulate the symptom in imagination and implement the coping strategy, again asking the patient to rate ease/success. Continue until the patient's rating of ease and success of use is high and stable.
   (b) When a coping strategy is difficult to practice within the session then:
      (i) clearly stipulate the required procedure in behavioural terms and conditions under which it is to be implemented;
      (ii) verify through feedback that the patient is fully aware of the strategy and conditions under which it should be used;
      (iii) practice this procedure in imagination;
      (iv) set self-directed *in vivo* practice as homework tasks.
5. Instruct the patient in how to monitor and record the implementation of the strategy. Set explicit and appropriate homework exercises involving the use of coping strategies in real life situations. Homework exercises should gradually become more complex and difficult.
6. During the next session verify that the strategy was implemented and assess its success through examination of records and by direct questioning. If the strategy was successful then reinforce the patient with praise and encouragement and give booster practice. If it was not implemented then return to stage 1. If it was not successful then assess the possible reasons, modify the intervention accordingly and

re-implement. If there is no improvement then select a new target symptom.
7. Implement at least two strategies for each symptom before selecting a new target symptom. Further strategies can also be added later if required.

Attempt to achieve a consistent and stable approach and not one characterised by short and general advice. Patients may require long and detailed training in coping methods before change is produced in their symptoms. It should be remembered that non-psychotic patients frequently hold irrational beliefs with great conviction which are difficult to modify, therefore psychotic patients can be expected to change at an even slower rate.

## Case example

Tom experienced unpleasant and hostile auditory hallucinations mainly describing his actions and his thoughts. They occurred when he was out of the house, in public places, in queues and at the shops. He would also experience these voices when alone and inactive at home, usually in the evening and at night. These experiences would make him feel frightened and angry. He also experienced feeling that other people could read his mind, this was especially true of teenagers whom he thought were "out to get him". Generally, he did not experience any such symptoms at home during the day, in the company of his parents with whom he lived or when at the day hospital which he attended twice a week. He found his experiences exceedingly distressing and consequently he avoided going out of the house if at all possible and he found the journey to the day hospital very difficult and frightening. He frequently failed to attend or occasionally he took a taxi which was a strain on his limited finances. At home he did little except watch the television and occasionally help his retired parents around the house. He tried to shout back and argue with the voices, especially when he was at home, and he would occasionally get into arguments with teenagers and schoolchildren while travelling to the day hospital. On one occasion Tom had hit a teenage boy while on the bus as he had thought that he was going to be attacked. Objectively, however, Tom's assault was unprovoked. Tom said that he did try to think of other things to distract himself but this was usually unsuccessful.

The first situation to be targeted was the experience of auditory hallucinations at home. These occurred mainly during the evenings and at night when he was alone in his room. It was first suggested that he should avoid spending long periods alone in his room during the evenings. As an alternative he should spend more time with his parents and if possible engage them in conversation. Goals were set for spending specified time periods with his parents and to attempt suitable conversation with them. This resulted in the reduction of time spent in the precipitating situation but Tom still experienced the voices when he went to bed. Coping in this situation was broken down into three elements:

1. reattributing the experience as illness-related and not due to a group of people gathering outside his window;

2. allowing himself to relax instead of getting angry and tense;
3. instructing himself not to respond to the voices but to continue with his relaxation.

Firstly, Tom was taught a quick version of autogenic relaxation which concentrated on "letting go" of tension, controlled breathing and self-instruction to relax. Secondly, Tom was taught to relabel the voices as illness-related. This involved using the onset of the auditory hallucinations as a stimulus to repeat relabelling statements. These statements were: "the voices aren't real", "they're a symptom of the illness", "they cannot hurt me". These statements were written down on a cue-card and Tom memorised them during the session. The therapist then simulated the auditory hallucinations in response to which Tom repeated aloud the three statements. After the first practice Tom rated on a 11-point scale (0 = "cannot do it" to 10 = "no trouble, completely successful") how easy he had found this. In fact he had found this task quite difficult (a score of 3) and he had muddled his statements. Practice continued until Tom correctly repeated the statements and scored at least 7 on three consecutive trials. The complete procedure was then repeated with Tom repeating the statements covertly instead of aloud and then again with Tom imagining the voices instead of the therapist simulating them.

The next stage was to use the successful repetition of the relabelling statements as a cue to implement relaxation. This again was practised under simulated conditions until a success criterion was achieved. Lastly, the maintenance and reality-test component was taught. Tom believed the voices came from people who were outside his window and were planning an imminent attack. By getting angry and shouting back at them he believed that he had prevented an actual physical attack. Distraction was unlikely to be successful unless this belief was challenged. Tom and the therapist agreed to put this belief to the test. If the voices were real and Tom's belief true then a failure to argue should result in an attack. If the therapist's view that the voices were a symptom of his illness was true then no attack should occur. The third element of the coping sequence were statements aimed at maintaining relaxation and preventing a reply to the voices, e.g., "If I just concentrate on my breathing, I'll be OK", "I mustn't reply". Tom's homework was to spend the evening in the presence of his parents and then to implement the coping sequence outlined above when he retired to his room.

When Tom was seen again 3 days later it transpired that this sequence had been partially successful. The first 2 nights he had managed not to shout back at the voices, but he had done so on the third night. Tom agreed that he had not been attacked and although his belief in the voices being real was still strong, he felt greatly relieved and much less concerned for his own safety. The difficulty with the programme appeared to be in maintaining distraction and physical relaxation over an extended period of time while not attending to the voices. Further distraction strategies were therefore required.

Tom was asked to think of an activity or situation that he liked doing or enjoyed. He chose having a meal in a favourite café in Blackpool. This was where he spent his holidays and the situation had a lot of positive memories for him. He was asked to describe the situation in detail while creating a mental image of himself having his favourite meal. This was practised until he could easily produce and maintain a mental image of the situation. The previous training procedure was then repeated with Tom switching his attention to this positive mental image after repeating the relaxation maintaining self-statement to himself. He was then instructed to use the extended procedure for coping with the hallucinations that occurred in the evenings.

This modified procedure proved much more successful in maintaining distraction.

A similar procedure was implemented to deal with the psychotic experiences Tom had while travelling to the day centre. Training in a similar package of coping strategies was performed with the therapist firstly verbalising the delusional ideas that people at the bus stop could read his thoughts, were talking about him and were going to "get him". These overt verbalisations were used as cues to implement the coping package, when the success criterion was achieved the procedure was repeated with Tom imagining the delusional thoughts. As homework Tom was instructed not to avoid travelling to the centre by public transport but to use this difficult situation as a training exercise for implementing the coping strategies. As before attention was focused on modifying the emotional and behavioural sequelae of the psychotic phenomena on the basis that these formed an emotional and behavioural complex which maintained the occurrence of the psychotic symptoms and were also strong inhibiters of appropriate on-going behaviour which compromised his quality of life.

It should be clear from this example that a detailed behavioural analysis of the patients symptomatology and systematic training in coping strategies is essential. It may also be the case that coping strategies and behavioural testing are not powerful enough to remove the delusional belief but may remove the emotional and behavioural consequences of that belief. For example another patient would experience auditory hallucinations of voices shouting obscenities. She experienced these on one occasion while attending a church social and became convinced that other attenders had heard the voices and believed that it was her blaspheming. She became convinced that she was being shunned because of these transgressions and decided that she could not attend any further meetings. Besides causing her considerable distress these meetings were her only social activity. The therapist accepted her beliefs as being possible and predicted that if she did attend a further meeting the other women would make their disapproval evident. An alternative explanation was also advanced and this was that the voices were part of her illness and that she had misinterpreted the social cues at the meeting because of her distress. This explanation would predict that if she attended further meetings and concentrated on controlling her anxiety there would be no social censure. Putting these two explanations to the test she found that she was welcomed to the meetings as before. In the week following she agreed that her belief had been wrong. A number of weeks later, however, she said that she was firmly convinced that the other women had heard the voices but this no longer caused her any distress and she continued to attend church meetings with evident enjoyment. In this case the hallucinations and their delusional interpretations were not permanently eradicated but the consequential emotional distress was alleviated and social withdrawal and isolation prevented.

## Potential problems and difficulties in implementation

To achieve success with this therapeutic strategy the patient must be engaged and maintained in treatment for a sufficient time to teach them the appropriate skills and to ensure that these skills are implemented appropriately and consistently. There are a number of potential problems that may arise with this patient population.

1. Initial engagement can be difficult and some time may be necessarily spent building up a personal relationship with the patient before assessment and treatment can be initiated. It should be remembered that schizophrenia frequently renders the sufferer intolerant of social stimulation. Hence the duration of sessions may, at least at first, be quite short. Recognition that the patient's experiences and their interpretation of them are very real to the patient will help to build rapport. Practical arrangements such as seeing the patient at home or at a day centre or drop in centre may also facilitate initial engagement.

2. Many patients may retain absolute conviction in their delusional beliefs. Since a confrontational approach is likely to discourage engagement attention should be focused on the negative emotional consequences of these experiences and the positive effect that the alleviation of such distress will have for the patient.

3. Since many patients have chronic illnesses the approach of psychiatric staff to the patient's self-report of their symptoms is frequently to ignore them. Hence the assessment and treatment procedure detailed here may have the effect of encouraging the patient to talk about their symptoms. It is therefore important to pay careful attention to the changes in contingencies and their consequences that this programme may bring about.

4. A time limited treatment programme may be inappropriate for some patients who will need involvement for an extended period of time. Other patients should be provided with regular booster sessions to maintain treatment benefits.

5. Symptom management programmes should be integrated with other intervention programmes to meet the individual needs of the patient. For example, it may be desirable to combine both the CSE programme with a Problem-Solving programme so as to address wider areas of functioning. Similarly interventions focused on living skills (Vaccaro and Roberts 1992) could be incorporated to expand the patient's behaviour repertoire and level of functioning.

6. Emotional difficulties such as depression are common in patients suffering from schizophrenia and may also need to be addressed.

7. Other factors may also affect the variation in symptom level. These may be internal and require pharmacological intervention or external such as the level of stress in the home environment and may require a psychosocial intervention with the patient's relatives (see Chapter 6).

8. Strategies for maintenance of coping skills should be programmed into the overall treatment approach, this may involve the collaboration of relatives or other direct care staff or psychiatric personnel.

CONCLUSIONS

In conclusion there is reasonable evidence that careful and systematic intervention designed to improve symptom management can result in improvements in drug resistant symptoms. These benefits, especially when integrated into a comprehensive treatment plan can improve the quality of life of patients suffering from schizophrenia.

REFERENCES

Adams, H.E., Malatesta, V., Brontley, P.J. and Turkat, I.D. (1981) Modification of cognitive processes: a case study of schizophrenia. *Journal of Consulting and Clinical Psychology*, **49**, 460–4.

Alford, B.A. (1986) Behavioural treatments of schizophrenic delusions: a single-case experimental analysis. *Behavior Therapy*, **17**, 637–44.

Alford, G.S. and Turner, S.M. (1976) Stimulus interference and conditioned inhibition of auditory hallucinations. *Journal of Behavior Therapy and Experimental Psychiatry*, **7**, 155–60.

Alford, G.S., Fleece, L. and Rothblum, E. (1982) Hallucinatory–delusional verbal-isations: modification in a chronic schizophrenic by self-control and cognitive restructuring. *Behavior Modification*, **6**, 421–35.

Anderson, L.T. and Alpert, M. (1974) Operant analysis of hallucination frequency in a hospitalised schizophrenic. *Journal of Behavior Therapy and Experimental Psychiatry*, **5**, 13–18.

Ayllon, T. and Haughton, E. (1964) Modification of symptomatic verbal behavior of mental patients. *Behaviour Research and Therapy*, **2**, 87–97.

Barrowclough, C. and Tarrier, N. (1992) *Families of Schizophrenic Patients: Cognitive Behavioural Intervention*, Chapman and Hall, London.

Barrowclough, C., Tarrier, N., Watts, S., Vaughn, C. and Freeman, H.L. (1985) *Information for Relatives about Schizophrenia*, North West Fellowship, Warrington.

Baskett, S.J. (1983) Tardive dyskinesia and treatment of psychosis after withdrawal of neuroleptics. *Brain Research Bulletin*, **11**, 173–4.

Beck, A.T. (1952) Successful out-patient psychotherapy of a chronic schizophrenic with a delusion based on borrowed guilt. *Psychiatry*, **15**, 305–12.

Belcher, T.L. (1988) Behavioural reduction of overt hallucinatory behaviour in chronic schizophrenics. *Journal of Behavior Therapy and Experimental Psychiatry*, **19**, 69–71.

Bental, R.P., Higson, P. and Lowe, C.F. (1987) Teaching self-instruction to chronic schizophrenic patients: efficacy and generalisation. *Behaviour Psychotherapy*, **15**, 58–76.

Birchwood, M. (1986) Control of auditory hallucinations through occlusion of monoaural auditory input. *British Journal of Psychiatry*, **149**, 104–7.

Birchwood, M., Smith J., Cochrane, R., Wetton, S. and Copestake, S. (1990) The social functioning scale: the development and validation of a scale of social adjustment for use in family intervention programmes with schizophrenic patients. *British Journal of Psychiatry*, **157**, 853–9.

Breier, A. and Strauss, J.S. (1983) Self-control in psychotic disorders. *Archives of General Psychiatry*, **40**, 1141–5.

Brenner, H.D. (1986) On the importance of cognitive disorders in treatment and rehabilitation. In: J. Strauss, W. Boker and H. D. Brenner (eds), *Psychosocial Treatment of Schizophrenia*, Hans Huber, Bern.

Brenner, H.D., Kraemer, S., Hermanutz, M. and Hodel, B. (1990) Cognitive treatments in schizophrenia. In: E.R. Straube and K. Hahlweg (eds), *Schizophrenia: Concepts Vulnerability and Intervention*, Springer-Verlag, Berlin.

Brett-Jones, J., Garety, P. and Hemsley, D. (1987) Measuring delusional experience: a method and its application. *British Journal of Clinical Psychology*, **26**, 257–65.

Bucher, B. and Fabricatore, J. (1970) Use of patient administered shock to suppress hallucinations. *Behavior Therapy*, **1**, 382–5.

Bulow, H., Oei, T.P.S. and Pinkey, B. (1979) Effects of contingent social reinforcement with delusional chronic schizophrenic men. *Psychological Reports*, **44**, 659–66.

Carr, V. (1988) Patients' techniques for coping with schizophrenia: an exploratory study. *British Journal of Medical Psychology*, **61**, 339–52.

Chadwick, P. and Lowe, F.L. (1991) The measurement and modification of delusional beliefs. *Journal of Consulting and Clinical Psychology*, **58**, 225–32.

Cohen, C.I. and Berk, B.S. (1985) Personal coping styles of schizophrenic out-patients. *Hospital and Community Psychiatry*, **36**, 407–10.

Curson D.A., Barnes, T.R.E., Bamber, R.W., Platt, S.D., Hirsch, S.R. and Duffy, J.D. (1985) Long term depot maintenance of chronic schizophrenic outpatients. *British Journal of Psychiatry*, **146**, 464–80.

Curson, D.A., Patel, M., Liddle, P.F. and Barnes, T.R.E. (1988) Psychiatric morbidity of a long stay hospital population with chronic schizophrenia and implications for future community care. *British Medical Journal*, **297**, 819–22.

Davis, J.M. (1975) Overview: maintenance therapy in psychiatry: I. Schizophrenia. *American Journal of Psychiatry*, **13**, 1237–54.

Davis, J.M., Schaffer, C.B., Killian, G.A., Kinard, C. and Chan, C. (1980) Important issues in the drug treatment of schizophrenia. *Schizophrenia Bulletin*, **6**, 70–87.

Davis, J.R., Wallace, C.J., Liberman, R.P. and Finch, B.E. (1976) The use of brief isolation to suppress delusional and hallucinatory speech. *Journal of Behavior Therapy and Experimental Psychiatry*, **7**, 269–75.

Erickson, E., Darnell, M.H. and Labeck, I. (1978) Belief treatment of hallucinatory behaviour with behavioural techniques. *Behavior Therapy*, **9**, 663–5.

Falloon, I.R.H. and Talbot, R.E. (1981) Persistent auditory hallucinations: coping mechanisms and implications for management. *Psychological Medicine*, **11**, 329–39.

Feder, R. (1982) Auditory hallucinations treated by radio headphones. *American Journal of Psychiatry*, **139**, 1188–90.

Fonagy, P. and Slade, P. (1982) Punishment vs negative reinforcement in the aversive conditioning of auditory hallucinations. *Behaviour Research and Therapy*, **20**, 483–92.

Fowler, D. and Morley, S. (1989) The cognitive–behavioural treatment of hallucinations and delusions: a preliminary study. *Behavioural Psychotherapy*, **17**, 267–82.

Gresen, R. (1974) The effects of instruction and reinforcement on a multifaceted self-control procedure in the modification and generalisation of behaviour in schizophrenia. Unpublished Ph.D. thesis, Bowling Green University (cited by Margolis and Shemberg, 1976).

Green, W.P., Glass, A. and O'Callaghan, M.A. (1980) Some implications of abnormal hemisphere interaction in schizophrenia. In: J. Gruzelier and P. Flor-Henry (eds), *Hemisphere Asymmetries and Psychopathology*, Macmillan, London.

Green, W.P., Hallett, S. and Hunter, M. (1983) Abnormal interhemispheric specialisations in schizophrenic and high risk children. In: P. Flor-Henry and J. Gruzelier (eds), *Laterality and Psychopathology*, Elsevier, Amsterdam.

Gross, G. (1986) Basic symptoms and coping behaviour in schizophrenia. In: J. Strauss, W. Boker and H.D. Brenner (eds), *Psychosocial Treatment of Schizophrenia*. Hans Huber, Bern.

Harrow, M. and Silverstein, M.L. (1977) Psychotic symptoms in schizophrenia after the acute phase. *Schizophrenia Bulletin*, **3**, 608–16.

Hartman, L.M. and Cashman, F.E. (1983) Cognitive–behavioural and psychophar-macological treatment of delusional symptoms: a preliminary report. *Behavioural Psychotherapy*, **11**, 50–61.

Hawton, K., Salkovskis, P.M., Kirk, J. and Clark, D.M. (1989) *Cognitive Behaviour Therapy for Psychiatric Problems*. Oxford University Press.

Horowitz, M.J. (1975) A cognitive model of hallucinations. *American Journal of Psychiatry*, **132**, 789–95.

Hole, R.W., Rush, A.J. and Beck, A.T. (1979) A cognitive investigation of schizophrenic delusions. *Psychiatry*, **42**, 312–19.

James, D. (1983) The experimental treatment of two cases of verbal hallucinations. *British Journal of Psychiatry*, **143**, 515–16.

Johnson, D.A.W., Ludlow, J.M., Street, K. and Taylor, R.D.W. (1987) Double blind comparison of half-dose and standard dose flupenthixol decanoate in the maintenance treatment of stabilised out-patient schizophrenics. *British Journal of Psychiatry*, **151**, 634–38.

Krawiecka, M., Goldberg, D. and Vaughan, M. (1977) A standardised psychiatric assessment scale for rating chronic psychotic patients. *Acta Psychiatrica Scandinavica*, **55**, 299–308.

Lamontagne, Y., Audet, N. and Elie, R. (1983) Thought stopping for delusions and hallucinations: a pilot study. *Behavioural Psychotherapy*, **11**, 177–84.

Leff, J.P. and Wing, J.K. (1971) Trial of maintenance therapy in schizophrenia. *British Medical Journal*, **iii**, 599–604.

Liberman, R.P., Teigan, J., Patterson, R. and Baker, V. (1973) Reducing delusional speech in chronic paranoid schizophrenics. *Journal of Applied Behavior Analysis*, **6**, 57–64.

Lukoff, D., Nuechterlein, K.H. and Ventura, J. (1986) Manual for Expanded Brief Psychiatric Rating Scale (BPRS). *Schizophrenia Bulletin*, **12**, 594–602.

Magaro, P.A., Johnson, M. and Boring, R. (1986) Information processing approaches to the treatment of schizophrenia. In: R.E. Ingram (ed.), *Information Processing Approaches to Clinical Psychology*, Academic, London.

Margolis, R. and Shemberg, K. (1976) Use of self-instruction for the elimination of psychotic speech. *Behavior Therapy*, **7**, 668–71.

Meichenbaum, D. and Cameron, R. (1973) Training schizophrenics to talk to themselves: a means of developing attentional control. *Behavior Therapy*, **4**, 515–34.

Meyes, A., Mercatons, M. and Sirota, A. (1976) Use of self-instruction for the elimination of psychotic speech. *Journal of Consulting and Clinical Psychology*, **44**, 480–2.

Milton, F., Patwa, V.K. and Hafner, J. (1978) Confrontation vs belief modification in persistently deluded patients. *British Journal of Medical Psychology*, **51**, 127–30.

Morley, S. (1987) Modification of auditory hallucinations: experimental studies of headphones and earplugs. *Behaviour Psychotherapy*, **15**, 240–51.

Nydegger, R.V. (1972) The elimination of hallucinatory and delusional behaviours by verbal conditioning and assertive training: a case study. *Journal of Behavior Therapy and Experimental Psychiatry*, **3**, 225–7.

Paul, G. and Lentz, R. (1977) *Psychological Treatment of Chronic Mental Patients. Milieu versus Social Learning Programmes*, Harvard University Press, Cambridge, Mass.

Schneider, S.J. and Pope, A.T. (1982) Neuroleptic-like electroencephalographic changes in schizophrenics through biofeedback. *Biofeedback and Self-Regulation*, **7**, 479–90.

Slade, P.D. (1972) The effects of systematic desensitisation auditory hallucinations. *Behaviour Research and Therapy*, **10**, 85–91.

Slade, P.D. (1973) The psychological investigation and treatment of auditory hallucinations: a second case report. *British Journal of Medical Psychology*, **46**, 293–6.

Slade, P.D. (1976) Towards a theory of auditory hallucinations: outline of an hypothetical four-factor model. *British Journal of Social and Clinical Psychology*, **15**, 415–23.

Silverstein, M.L. and Harrow, M. (1978) First rank symptoms in the post acute schizophrenic: a follow-up study. *American Journal of Psychiatry*, **135**, 1481–6.

Spaulding, W.D., Storms, L., Goodrich, V. and Sullivan, M. (1986) Application of experimental psychopathology in psychiatric rehabilitation. *Schizophrenia Bulletin*, **12**, 560–77.

Tarrier, N. (1987) An investigation of residual psychotic symptoms in discharged schizophrenic patients. *British Journal of Clinical Psychology*, **26**, 141–3.

Tarrier, N. and Main, C. (1986) Applied relaxation training (ART) with patients suffering from generalised anxiety and panic attacks: the efficacy of a learnt coping strategy on subjective reports. *British Journal of Psychiatry*, **149**, 330–6.

Tarrier, N., Harwood, S., Yusopoff, L., Beckett, R. and Baker, A. (1990) Coping Strategy Enhancement (CSE): a method of treating residual schizophrenic symptoms. *Behavioural Psychotherapy* **18**, 283–93.

Tress, K.H., Bellenis, C., Brownlow, J.M., Livinston, G. and Leff, J.P. (1987) The Present State Examination Change rating scale. *British Journal of Psychiatry*, **150**, 201–7.

Turner, S., Herson, M. and Bellack, A. (1977) Effects of social disruption, stimulus interference and aversive conditioning on auditory hallucinations. *Behaviour Modification*, **1**, 249–58.

Vaccaro, J.V. and Roberts, L. (1992) Teaching social and coping skills. In M. Birchwood and N. Tarrier (eds), *Innovations in the Psychological Management of Schizophrenia*, Wiley, Chichester, pp. 103–14.

Watts, F.N., Powell, G.E. and Austin, S.V. (1973) The modification of abnormal beliefs. *British Journal of Medical Psychology*, **46**, 359–63.

Weingaertner, A.H. (1971) Self-administered aversive stimulation with hallucinating hospitalised schizophrenics. *Journal of Consulting and Clinical Psychology*, **36**, 422–9.

West, L.J. (1962) A general theory of hallucinations and dreams. In: L.J. West, (ed.), *Hallucinations*, Grune & Stratton, New York.

Wing, J.K., Cooper, J.E. and Sartorius, N. (1974) *Measurement and Classification of Psychiatric Symptoms: an Instruction Manual for the PSE and Catego Programme*, Cambridge University Press.

## Chapter 6

# Models of Continuing Care

TONY LAVENDER AND FRANK HOLLOWAY

## INTRODUCTION

This chapter reviews models of continuing care for people suffering from severe long-term mental health problems. The discussion is therefore not limited to services for those who are diagnosed as suffering from schizo-phrenia, although invariably this is the most frequent diagnosis among samples of the "old" and "new" long-stay inpatients and the "new long term" living in the community (Wainwright, Holloway and Brugha, 1988; Patrick et al., 1989; Clifford et al., 1991).

The chapter begins with a historical overview of community care services. Developments during the 1980s are discussed, and concerns commonly expressed about current provision are reviewed. The essential components of a continuing care service are then presented. The chapter closes with an attempt to identify future trends. The focus is on mental health services in Britain. Similar trends in policy and provision can be identified throughout the West (Mangen, 1988) and relevant literature from Europe, North America and Australia is presented.

## THE HISTORY OF MENTAL HEALTH CARE IN THE COMMUNITY

Public mental health services originated as a philanthropic response to the needs of "pauper lunatics". During the early nineteenth century asylums functioned as therapeutic institutions. "Moral treatment" in small, humanely-run, institutions produced impressive discharge and cure rates (Bockhoven, 1954). From the mid-1800s the increasingly extensive network of local asylums entered what has been described as their "long sleep".

Patient numbers expanded rapidly, and cost containment became a major priority (Scull, 1979). Even during this era of "custodial care" there was some interest in the care of patients released into the community, as evidenced by the founding of the Mental Aftercare Association in 1879. Since the 1920s there has been a progressive move towards "community care", gathering pace following the Second World War (Martin, 1984a; Ramon, 1988).

A variety of intellectual undercurrents have shaped the community care movement (Ramon, 1988). An important factor was the "psychologisation" of everyday life that was associated with increased interest in Freud's thought which began during the 1920s and gathered momentum during the Second World War. The idea that everyone was potentially abnormal given adequate stress gained currency, and this may have increased tolerance within the community towards abnormal behaviour (Ramon, 1988). The therapeutic community movement stemmed from attempts by military psychiatrists to rehabilitate psychiatric casualties of war by engaging them in the treatment process (Bion, 1989). The movement began to have an impact on traditional mental hospitals, which had left local authority control with the founding of the NHS in 1948, during the 1950s. Medical Superintendents introduced an "open door" policy, which meant both literally opening the doors of wards within the hospital and figuratively making discharge (and readmission) of patients easier and more frequent (Ramon, 1988). In some hospitals rehabilitation wards were established, and the then novel techniques of occupational therapy were applied (Bennett, 1983).

At the same time psychiatric hospitals, and other institutions, were criticised as environments that produced apathy and physical and mental deterioration among residents (Barton, 1959). The highly complex relationship between social environment and psychiatric disorder has subsequently been the subject of considerable research (e.g. Wing and Brown, 1970; Vaughn and Leff, 1976; Brown and Harris, 1978; Goldstein and Caton, 1983; Falloon and Liberman, 1983; Shepherd, 1988). However, this body of empirical evidence has been less influential than the simplistic message that institutions are both dehumanising and largely responsible for the disabilities of their residents (Jones and Fowles, 1984).

During the 1960s and 1970s a series of scandals broke out when the quality of care in mental illness and mental handicap hospitals was found to have deteriorated to an unacceptable degree (Martin, 1984b). Common themes were identified in the official enquiries that resulted; these included the isolation of institutions and the staff groups within them, a failure of professional leadership and general management, lack of resources and inadequate training of staff (Martin, 1984b). These scandals served "to reinforce the developing view that the large institutions were self-evidently harmful" (Thornicroft and Bebbington, 1989). It is not, however, clear that the underlying causes of institutional failure have been adequately understood by critics of the institution.

A further medicalisation of mental illness followed the introduction of effective drug treatment for depression and schizophrenia during the 1950s (Scull, 1984). Psychiatry moved into the District General Hospital (DGH). This move was predicated on the belief by politicians that major mental illnesses could now be cured (Scull, 1984, p. 81). Outpatient and day-care expanded, although the community support available to patients and carers in the new pattern of services was often inadequate (Brown et al., 1966). Community psychiatric nursing (CPN) emerged in the 1950s and has subsequently expanded steadily to become an essential component of every District Psychiatric Service. Conflicting models for CPN services emerged. There remains an unresolved tension between the CPN as a member of a multidisciplinary psychiatric team and as an independent practitioner working in primary care (Royal College of Psychiatrists, 1980; Conway-Nicholls and Elliott, 1982; Martin, 1984a). The available evidence does not, however, favour the independent practitioner model (Woof and Goldberg, 1988).

During the 1960s and early 1970s a rejection of traditional concepts of "mental illness" was articulated in the vivid writings of the "antipsychiatrists" (Sedgwick, 1982). Hospitalisation for episodes of "acute mental distress" was rejected in favour of psychotherapeutic approaches and communal living, in which sufferers would be supported by the lay people with whom they lived. More recently the "primary consumer" movement has had an increasingly influential voice. This may become an attempt to liberate the subjects of a system that is seen to serve the needs of the professional rather than the user, adopting the ideas and terminology of "antipsychiatry" (Brown, 1981; Chamberlain, 1988). The concept of empowerment of service users and the practice of advocacy are becoming increasingly significant within mental health services (Royal College of Psychiatrists, 1989). The necessity for an advocate to be independent of the service system has been stressed (Sang, 1989). There is growing interest in incorporating the views of users into the planning process (Kingsley and Towell, 1988). This occasionally takes tangible form.

Normalisation has been increasingly influential amongst managers and clinicians in services for people with severe learning difficulties and more recently the mentally ill (Kingsley and Towell, 1988). The principles of normalisation (Wolfensberger, 1972), or social role valorisation (Wolfensberger, 1983) are the subject of intense controversy (Garety, 1988). There has been no dispassionate review in the proposition that "all human services (and particularly those serving people who are subjected to discrimination, are marginalised or devalued) should aim to enable users to reach as valued a social position as possible" (Wainwright, Holloway and

Brugha, 1988). Normalisation principles have been developed into a very powerful training tool that can also serve as a framework for service evaluation (Wolfensberger and Glen, 1973; O'Brien and Tyne,1981; Wolfensberger and Thomas, 1983; Kingsley, Towell and McAusland, 1985).

One common element of the community care movement has been a tendency to deny the severity and persistence of the disabilities experienced by many people who suffer from long-term mental health problems. The terminology used to identify sufferers from "long-term mental health problems" to "chronic mental illness" is a cause of controversy and confusion (Bachrach, 1988; Lavender and Holloway, 1988). Illness-language may be seen as devaluing and excessively "medical". In reality contemporary psychiatric thinking emphasises the interaction between the biological, the psychological and the social (Falloon and Liberman, 1983; Wing, 1983).

There also appears to have been a rather naive view of what the terms "community" and "community care" actually mean (Hawks, 1975; Abrams, 1977). Enthusiasm for community-based work and the use of non-specialist resources was prevalent among the increasing number of social workers recruited and trained to staff the burgeoning social services departments that were formed in 1971 (Martin, 1984a). Ironically this anti-professional stance coincides with the politically powerful perspective that in some sense the community should be providing for its own. By implication responsible citizens should be so arranging their lives and finances that they can receive support from friends and relatives and purchase professional care when the need arises.

Radical commentators have pointed out that in reality a major motivating behind community care has been the fiscal crisis of welfare that affects all Western countries (Jones and Fowles, 1984; Scull, 1984). This crisis has led to a general policy emphasis towards targeting resources at those who are deemed to need them most. Financial considerations have also played a large part in the decision to close hospitals.

CONTINUING CARE IN THE 1980s: INFLUENCES AND FAILURES

The pace of change in mental health services in Britain accelerated rapidly during the 1980s (Ramon, 1988). A small number of psychiatric hospitals actually closed, and plans for more closures were energetically pursued. The development of the "dowry", a financial mechanism that allowed money to move with patients discharged into the community, was highly significant (Mahoney, 1988). However, hospital inpatient services continued to consume more than 80% of Hospital and Community Health Services revenue (Taylor and Taylor, 1989). Despite the isolated examples of cooperation between the health service and local authority social service departments that could be identified (Audit Commision, 1986), Government initiatives to improve inter-agency working by means of joint finance largely failed. Joint finance seems in particular to have bypassed the needs of the mentally ill. The proportion of social service department expenditure devoted to the mentally ill increased but remained extremely low (HMSO, 1989a; Taylor and Taylor, 1989).

## Legislative changes

The British 1983 Mental Health Act, largely a product of libertarian concerns over compulsory detention in hospital, required local authorities to train "Approved Social Workers" who would make assessments for admission and were charged with considering alternative sources of help in the community. Although it offered some encouragement to the rediscovery of a mental health specialism within social services, the Act did nothing concrete to encourage community-based services (Ramon, 1988).

Much more influential on the pattern of provision, particularly but not exclusively for the elderly, was a change in social security regulations. This resulted in an explosion in the use of supplementary benefit board and lodging monies to subsidise people living in private and voluntary residential and nursing homes. Government monies became available to pay charges for residential care, up to a stipulated limit for a locality. These rules may have acted as a perverse incentive against the development of domiciliary services by health and social service authorities (Audit Commission, 1986). There is evidence that the need to maximise revenue from welfare benefits may have influenced the plans to provide some British mental hospitals destined for closure (Mahoney, 1988; NUPRD, 1989).

## Problems with community care

The policy of community care attracted vociferous criticism (Scull, 1984). The National Schizophrenia Fellowship (NSF), an advocacy group composed largely of carers, described the realities of community care as "The Sham Behind the Slogan" (NSF, 1984). The NSF perspective was one of the relatively frequent tragic stories of individual neglect and family suffering. Examples cited include sons killing their mothers during a psychotic breakdown, and severely disabled individuals apparently being left to wander the streets or live in unsuitable boarding house accommodation (Taylor and Taylor, 1989).

The report "Making a Reality of Community Care" (Audit Commission, 1986) reviewed progress towards the British Government's stated objective of promoting community care for the elderly, mentally ill, mentally handi-capped and people with physical disability. It found that progress towards community care had been slowest for mentally ill people. The reduction in NHS residential provision had outstripped the build-up of community resources. There were gross geographical variations in services. Funding arrangements both for the NHS and Local Authorities worked against the development of community services, with local authorities that are progressive actually suffering financial penalties. There was a lack of bridging finance to ease the transition between hospital-and-community-based services. Joint planning between Health and Local Authorities was in disarray, with fragmented responsibility for the development of community-based services. Organisational arrangements for delivering community care at the local level were exceedingly complex, with the many agencies involved working to quite different priorities. Staffing arrangements for the new services were inadequate. There had been a failure to address training needs both within the declining institution and in the new services. A decade of persuasion and exhortation from central government following the White Paper *Better Services for the Mentally Ill* (HMSO, 1975) had had little impact on the delivery of community-care services. The Audit Commission consequently recommended that a new organisational framework be developed that would remedy these problems.

This powerful critique of the organisational aspects of community care policies serves as a background for discussion of the practical problems of community care for people with long-term mental health problems. Com-plaints have included inadequate resources; perverse incentive towards residential care; poor quality of care and quality of life for chronically men-tally ill people; inappropriate diversion of mentally ill people into the criminal justice system; community care policies causing homelessness; community care policies resulting in unacceptable family burden; and poor coordination of care to the individual patient/client.

There is very little systematic data available on the quality of the supports that have been provided to people with long-term mental health problems, even the special group who return to the community after prolonged periods of inpatient care. Indeed there has been a startling lack of clarity about what should be provided. For patients who have been in hospital discharge planning may take place but may be naive, unrealistic and fail to take account of the range of social and medical needs experienced by patients (Caton, Goldstein and Serrano, 1984). Day-care, seen as an essen-tial component of service, varies in quantity throughout Britain and is also probably of very variable quality (Brewin, Wing and Mangen, 1988; Wainwright, Holloway and Brugha, 1988). There is however no doubt that day care users value what is provided (Holloway, 1989).

For many former psychiatric hospital residents in America, community care came to mean "transinstitutionalisation" rather than "deinstitutionalisation" (Mangen, 1988). Patients regarded as institutionally dependent and/or untreatable were discharged into non-psychiatric nursing homes. This has been particularly true for the elderly (Talbott, 1988). Poor quality of care has been documented in the nursing home sector in America and West Germany (Brown, 1985; Kunze, 1985). A controlled trial of nursing home care versus traditional inpatient care for elderly mentally ill residents of Veterans' Administration Hospitals found that the decreased costs of nursing home care were achieved at the expense of poorer clinical outcome for the patients (Linn et al., 1985). In America less dependent patients have moved into Board and Care Homes, which may in some cases provide an acceptable alternative (Lamb, 1979). However, "For the long-term hospitalised patient, the move [from hospital to community] is usually into a boarding home facility.... These facilities are for the most part like small long-term state hospital wards isolated from the community. One is overcome by the depressing atmosphere ... because of the passivity, isolation and inactivity of the residents" (Lamb and Goertzel, 1971).

The scant available information suggests that most people are glad to have left hospital, whatever dissatisfactions they may have with their current situation (Johnstone et al., 1984; Kay and Legg, 1986; Lehman, Possidente and Hawker, 1986; Gibbons and Butler, 1987; Perkins, King and Hollyman, 1989). American studies into the quality of life of people with long-term mental health problems have indicated that severe difficulties are experienced in a variety of life domains (Lehman, 1983). Outcomes of relocation for former long-stay hospital residents are extremely variable. Anecdotal evidence suggests that those who were best-adjusted to life in the hospital, with a secure niche within the hospital community and relatively high status within the patient hierarchy, fare relatively badly (Marlowe, 1976; Holloway et al., 1988).

## Community care and prisons

It has been claimed that the decrease in the numbers of long-stay and acute psychiatric inpatient beds in Britain has resulted in an increase in the numbers of mentally disordered people in prison (Rollin, 1977; Bluglass, 1988; Scannell, 1989). Although individual patients may have been rejected by catchment area psychiatric services, often because of difficulty in containing severely disturbed behaviour within the District General Hospital (DGH) inpatient unit or a shortage of inpatient beds, there is no evidence of an excess of psychotic illnesses among prisoners (Coid, 1984). A further study of psychiatric morbidity in the prison population is under way

(Bluglass, 1988). This may show a marked increase in the prevalence of psychosis amongst prisoners on remand. Reluctance by catchment area psychiatrists, particularly those working in DGHs rather than mental hospitals, to accept mentally disordered remand prisoners for treatment has been documented (Coid, 1988a). Prisoners with long term mental health problems and severe social disabilities were particularly likely to be rejected. It would appear that neither the Regional Secure units that were opened for the more difficult mentally abnormal offenders nor contemporary DGH acute units can adequately address the needs of people with severe and long-term problems.

Lack of appropriate long-term residential provision, including long-term hospital care, may well have led to patients with severe illnesses or continuing vulnerability being discharged without adequate support and subsequently coming to the notice of services by offending. Coid (1988b) noted the desperate lengths some chronically disabled individuals went to in order to receive care. Attitudes of staff towards mentally disordered offenders vary markedly, and there is evidence that patients may be inappropriately labelled as psychopathic, personality disordered or violent as part of the process of rejection by services (Coid, 1988b).

## Homelessness

Homelessness among the mentally ill in the USA has been a major political issue (David, 1988). The reported prevalence of schizophrenia among samples of homeless persons has varied from 2% to 37% (Susser, Struening and Conover, 1989). A careful study of men admitted to municipal shelters in New York identified 17% as having a definite or probable diagnosis of psychosis. A firm diagnosis of schizophrenia was made in 8%, while 58% had a history of substance abuse (Susser, Struening and Conover, 1989). Shelters for homeless people have been described as "open asylums", which accept people who lack any relationship with traditional support systems (Bassuk, Rubin and Lauriat, 1984). These people are not being adequately helped by local psychiatric services (Lamb, 1984), or other social services agencies (Bassuk, Rubin and Lauriat, 1984). Consequently specialised treatment services for the homeless have been advocated (Jones, 1986; Susser, Struening and Conover, 1989).

There is evidence that psychosis and alcohol abuse are common among users of night shelters and the few remaining large homeless hostels in Britain (Weller et al., 1987; Timms, 1989). There is, however, controversy over the relationship between the decline in hospital beds for the mentally ill and the well-documented increase in homelessness among the mentally ill in Britain and the United States (Garety and Toms, 1990). A causative relationship has been argued (Weller, 1986), although a review of the case notes of any large psychiatric hospital with a reception centre in the catchment area is likely to identify patients who became long-stay decades ago after prolonged periods of homelessness. In England and Wales the discharge of patients from inpatient psychiatric care who are "Homeless and Vulnerable" under the 1977 Housing Act, and therefore liable to be offered temporary accommodation by local authority housing departments, is a part of everyday clinical practice in certain inner-city areas. Although there is an undoubted lack of specialised non-hospital residential accommodation for the mentally ill, the fact that former hospital residents become homeless is largely a reflection of the general housing crisis in Britain.

## Family burden

Community care implies to some not care "in the community" but care "by the community" (Ramon, 1988). In effect this may mean shifting the burden of care from the state to relatives (MacCarthy, 1988). This is despite evidence that the pattern of community supports is changing, with a decline in the numbers of people living with or close to relatives, a decline in traditional neighbourhoods, increasing isolation among some minorities and demographic changes altering the balance of carers to those in need (Audit Commission, 1986, p. 10). Early studies into community-oriented services indicated that this pattern of care was associated with an increased level of burden among relatives compared with traditional services which responded to disturbed behaviour by prolonged, even life-long, hospital admission (Grad and Sainsbury, 1968; Hoenig and Hamilton, 1969). More recent studies of highly community-oriented services that attempt to minimise usage of hospital beds have shown that these services either result in similar levels of burden compared to contemporary hospital-oriented practice (Fenton, Tessier and Struening, 1979) or are associated with decreased burden (Test and Stein, 1980; Hoult, 1986) It appears that the standard psychiatric service of the 1970s and 1980s offered poor support following an inpatient admission, in contrast to the community-oriented services that provided long-term support to the sufferer and carers, including appropriate intervention in crises.

## The coordination of care

One area of particular concern has been the lack of continuity of care for chronically mentally ill people, who are faced with a complex and confusing service system. One solution was the introduction of "case

management" services. These aim to improve the continuity and coordination of care, its accessibility, accountability and efficiency (Intagliata,
1982; Clifford and Craig, 1988; Renshaw, 1988; Kanter, 1989). Given the
well-documented reluctance of staff working in the community to address
the needs of the chronically mentally ill (Borus, 1981; Mollica, 1983),
opinion also began to favour the use of specialised "continuing care"
teams to coordinate care for the people with long-term and socially
disabling mental illnesses who lived within a defined geographical area
(Holloway, 1988; Lehman, 1989). The "continuing care team" and its relationship to case management are discussed in more detail below and in
Muijen (1992).

In Britain, experimental "community care" projects were shown to
decrease the need by frail elderly people for local authority residential care
and to delay admission into long-term hospital care. Social worker case
managers were employed who held budgets that could purchase paid
helpers who provided practical and emotional support (Challis and Davis,
1986). This important finding, which is not strictly relevant to mental
health services, was to shape subsequent government thinking about
community care for the whole range of client groups (HMSO, 1989a,
1989b).

### Policy developments

The 1980s closed with major British Government initiatives affecting both
community care and the NHS (HMSO, 1989a, 1989b). The community-care
proposals identified local authority social services departments as the
agency with lead responsibility for all community care client groups. This
appears unrealistic since in 1989 the local authority spending in England
and Wales on the mentally ill was 1/36th that of the National Health
Service (Taylor and Taylor, 1989). To confuse matters further the proposals
made a distinction between an individual's needs for "health" care, which
remained an NHS responsibility, and their "social" care, the responsibility
of the local social services authority. This distinction makes little sense to
those working within health services who have for many years realised
that mental health problems are the result of an interaction between
"social" and "health" domains. Effective treatment and care therefore
requires a programme of interventions that include both "social" and
"health" components. By working together local service providers might
mitigate the unfortunate consequences of the artificial health/social care
divide. Without such cooperation it is conceivable that the health service
contribution to community care will actually decrease, as providers
retrench to traditional bed-oriented styles of working.

A major aim of policy was to make services more cost-effective. To this end the purchaser of services (commissioning health authority or local authority social services department) was separated from the service provider (HMSO, 1989a, 1989b). The community-care proposals envisaged a "mixed economy of care" within which providers in the statutory, private and voluntary sector would compete. The relationship between purchaser and provider was to be regulated by service contracts. The long-term efficacy of this policy is open to doubt (Knapp, 1988). Contracting for services for the mentally ill has been markedly successful in a demonstrative project in the USA (Stein, Diamond and Factor, 1990). It is however, unlikely that services will have much of a market from which to choose. Reliance on private sector providers, working in isolation to tight budgets, must in any case be a cause of concern given experience in the USA (Mollica, 1983; Brown, 1985; Talbott 1988).

It has been argued that a central authority planning and directing a service system should act as a contractor of services rather than a service provider because any provider will substitute the needs of its employees for the needs of its clients as the organisation's primary goal (Stein, Diamond and Factor, 1990). This is not particularly plausible. There is a danger that if the purchaser/provider distinction is adhered to rigidly those in direct contact with people in need might be removed from the planning process. Purchasers would then lack the relevant information about what to buy. Effective organisational change requires the involvement of the people who must implement it (Georgiades and Phillimore, 1975), and direct care staff are vital stakeholders in the system. Their voice should be heard within the planning process, along with the voices of the consumers and carers (NIMH, 1987). Distancing providers from planning may result in the deprofessionalisation of community-care services and an increased split between hospital and community care. One possible way forward is for commissioners and providers to come together to plan services and agree arrangements for the monitoring and evaluation of services.

## COMPONENTS OF CONTINUING CARE

A number of publications have set out in a programmatic fashion the components of an ideal "continuing care" service (MIND, 1983; Richmond Fellowship, 1983; NIMH 1987). However, despite numerous examples of good practice, there are few blueprints available for a comprehensive service that can readily be copied. (An interesting exception is the model developed in Madison, USA to provide a comprehensive service for schizophrenic patients living in an affluent urban/rural community (Stein, Diamond and Factor; 1990).) Components of the service that can be confidently identified include a planning structure; adequate information systems; multidisciplinary teams to organise, coordinate and in part provide care; structured day activities; residential services; and access to care during crises. Other significant elements of a comprehensive service include support for carers, access to welfare rights advice and advocacy systems.


## Service planning

The development of high quality services requires leadership and clarity of vision. This has often been lacking partly because of the complex needs of the "continuing care client" and partly because of current interagency and interprofessional rivalries. Planning must involve all the relevant stakeholders (NIMH, 1987; Kingsley and Towell, 1988) which means that a planning group should be multidisciplinary and bring together both users and the relevant agencies. To be effective the group must include people who are innovative, understand the workings of the local health and social services, have the means to make plans a reality and have a direct knowledge of the needs of the client group. Members must also have the time and ability to undertake the necessary strategic and operational planning tasks. These range from developing a "vision" for the service to the minutiae of opening a project (see Wooff (1992) for a full review).

Commentators in the United States have argued that a central authority should be responsible for planning the service system, with responsibility for all patients in the catchment area and control over public monies for the client group (NIMH, 1987; Lehman, 1989; Stein, Diamond and Factor, 1990). In Britain, health authorities (responsible for "health" component of the community care) must assist local social services authorities (responsible for the "social" component) in the production of a "Community Care Plan" (HMSO, 1989a), but mechanisms for this joint planning are left to local negotiation.

Early on in the planning process the "philosophy" or aspirations of the service should be defined and an outline of its future shape should be produced. Differences between planning group members in their views about the nature of "long-term mental illness" or "severe mental health problems" should be acknowledged and as far as possible resolved at this stage. The subsequent service plans should be based on an appreciation of the local epidemiology and take account of existing provision. They should reflect local geography, including such mundane factors as the patterns of public transport, and should have a realistic chance of acceptance given local circumstances. Wide consultation should follow, with adjustment of plans in the light of reasoned comment. The opinions and support of those involved in implementing the plans should be sought.

## Information systems

Health authorities in Britain are now required to maintain a register of patients suffering from mental illness who are in need of continuing health and social care (HMSO, 1989a). Existing services lack adequate information systems. A register of those in need would seem to be an appropriate starting point to the planning process (Wing, 1972), and a potentially important mechanism for ensuring that people do not fall through the cracks of a complex service system. Traditional psychiatric case registers have contributed much to the epidemiological understanding of mental illnesses (see, for example, Wing and Hailey (1972), Gibbons, Jennings and Wing, (1984) and Walsh (1985)). These case registers were somewhat cumbersome, and were certainly not designed with the needs of practitioners and managers in mind. Technological advances have made it possible to develop "tailor-made" information systems based on micro-computers (Shepherd, 1988). A number of interesting projects have attempted to utilise this emerging technology to monitor the activity of a service system and the pattern of service contacts by individuals and to act as an aid to care planning (Fagin and Purser, 1986; Gibbons, 1986; Taylor and Bhumgara, 1989; Henderson, 1990). The introduction of a nationwide network of computerised registers of "people in need" is, however, fraught with both ethical and practical problems. The civil-libertarian aspects of being included on a register of vulnerable people, which might have serious implications for a person's future prospects of employment and access to financial services, have not been clearly addressed.

There is little difficulty in identifying data that might usefully be included on a register. The major stumbling block to the development of a clinically-relevant register is the amount of time required to input the data (Taylor and Bhumgara, 1989). This might suggest to the sceptic that registers should be as unambitious in scope as possible, merely including very basic sociodemographic, diagnostic and service contact data. Maintaining even a limited data-set is a formidable task. It is technically feasible for registers to serve other functions, including the facilitation of report writing and the assessment of the outcome of service contact (Taylor and Bhumgara, 1989). This technology currently appears to work best in the hands of enthusiasts who produce a system designed to meet local needs. To date no computerised system has been shown to be useful in more than one locality or over an extended period of time.

## The continuing care team

An effective multi-disciplinary team with a clear system for coordinating care is now seen as the hub of any service for people with long-term mental health problems (Holloway, 1988; Lehman, 1989; Stein, Diamond and Factor, 1990). This "continuing care" team needs to be multi-disciplinary because the client's needs are invariably multi-faceted, requiring expert assessment and intervention in social, psychological and medical areas. No single profession has the range of skills to provide an overall package of high quality care. It would be impossible to train a generic mental health worker to have an adequate level of knowledge and skills to intervene across the whole spectrum of needs. Good care occurs when the multidisciplinary team works together with the client to assess needs and priorities and then plan and implement a programme of care. This programme must be reviewed and revised regularly, if necessary over many years.

The current panacea for the ills of community care is the case manager. A number of potential models of case management exist (Clifford and Craig, 1988; Bachrach, 1989). The term case management is not well thought of by user groups. People dislike being identified as a case. Key working has been suggested as an alternative, although it may not adequately convey the range of responsibilities that the literature generally assigns to the case manager. The concept of the continuing care team fits well with the development of a case management system.

In order to carry out the case management function the team needs to organise itself to provide a coordinated package of care to each client. Thus a comprehensive assessment of the client's needs should come first. Assessment should include life skills (cooking, budgeting, personal hygiene, laundering, etc.), symptomatology and how it affects the client's life, social circumstances (housing, employment, social support and social life) and finances (Watts and Lavender, 1984). A number of team members will usually be involved in the assessment, including the person who will go on to function as the case manager (or "key worker"). The assessment will enable a package of care to be devised which will include therapy, treatment, advice and support in the areas of identified need. The case manager will coordinate this package of care and usually offer some direct care. The case manager inevitably therefore straddles the purchaser/provider divide.

The case manager will often involve other members of the continuing care team in the provision of care, but will also have to ensure that other agencies (e.g. the housing department, benefits offices, sheltered employers, adult education services) make their contribution. Staff must develop positive, supportive relationships with clients, as well as teaching them practical survival skills in real-life settings (Stein and Test, 1980). The service needs to be responsive 24 hours a day to requests from clients and carers (Finlay-Jones, 1983). A policy of assertive outreach is required to prevent people from falling through the cracks in the system. An important function of the case manager is to monitor the success of the package of care that was initially devised, and, with advice from the client and other members of the continuing care team, make any alterations that are required.

The team base, from which the case management system will operate, can provide a place where the client and other agencies involved in the care package can meet to coordinate and review their activities. The process of reviewing the function of the team is clearly central to the provision of a high-quality service. Clifford et al. (1989) provide an overview of the methods that have been used to monitor quality of care. Service management, care practices and treatment outcome all require evaluation. The QUARTZ system attempts to intervene at an organisational level to ensure the commitment and involvement of both managerial and direct care staff in the process of evaluation (Clifford et al. 1989). It also provides a set of evaluative schedules.

The team itself should offer its members both professional advice and a supportive group of colleagues who can help them deal with the personal stresses that are integral to work with a disadvantaged and disabled client group. Such support should help avoid the problems of staff "burn-out" and the high turnover of staff which often prevents teams from providing the long-term coordinated care that is an essential component of a high quality service (Test and Stein, 1980). Issues of recruitment, retention and career development are of crucial importance in all forms of community mental health care.

An important adjunct to any continuing care service is a strong system of client advocacy. Sang (1989) has described a number of working models. These have as a common element the activities of an individual (the advocate) who acts on behalf of or with the client to help obtain the best possible care, and helps make the client's wishes known to service providers. Many standard lists of the case management tasks include the role of advocate. This shows a misunderstanding of advocacy, since the advocate must always be independent of the services.

The model of the continuing care team put forward in this section argues against a strict distinction between purchasers and providers of services. Effective coordination of an agreed package of care is more than a bureaucratic exercise. It requires the active involvement of workers who have developed a therapeutic relationship with the client (Kanter, 1989).

Community-based teams operating in this way can be highly effective in preventing hospital admission and are generally preferred by clients and carers when compared with more traditional services (Stein and Test, 1980; Hoult, 1986). It is, however, important to emphasise that continuous care teams can only complement other elements of the service system. Like case management, the team is no panacea for community care. Forming and sustaining a team presents a considerable challenge to service managers, who must both offer the necessary support and guidance and allow the team to develop an identity that crosses traditional professional boundaries.

## Structured day activities

Work plays a central role in the lives of most people. Employment not only has "manifest" functions (e.g. monetary benefits), but also significant "latent" functions (e.g. structuring time, providing shared experiences and social contacts and enforcing activity) (Jahoda, 1981). Unemployment may lead to apathy, loss of social contact and loss of self-esteem (Warr, 1984). The Three Hospitals Study, which investigated the relationship between the quality of care and the clinical status of women diagnosed as suffering from schizophrenia, found that the more time patients spent doing nothing the more apathetic and withdrawn the patients were (Wing and Brown, 1970). Changes in the social environment were associated with changes in negative psychotic symptoms.

A key element in the influential "Fountain House" philosophy of psychosocial rehabilitation is the significance of productive activity and the opportunity for gainful employment for even the most disabled psychiatric client (Beard, Propst and Malamud, 1982). Any continuing care service should address users' needs for employment (in the sense of opportunities for paid work). A range of employment opportunities are required from access to open employment, through sheltered placements in ordinary firms to specialist sheltered work schemes (Pilling, 1988). Numerous isolated examples of good practice exist; a recent MIND publication listed over 300 work schemes currently operating in Britain (Stuart, 1990). Overall, however, provision is poor. Innovative and successful schemes reflect the local economy, and have tended to move away from the light industrial assembly work of traditional Industrial Therapy. Opportunities for training are also vital, and must take account of the particular problems of people with psychiatric disabilities, who may require additional support and time to complete a training scheme. In general it is important that such services are locally based, enable clients in valued work and, as far as possible, help them integrate with "ordinary" members of the community (Pilling, 1988). The location and appearance of sheltered work provision must be appropriate to its function. The product range must be marketable, and be sufficiently interesting to produce that a workforce is retained. Work schemes must assess their clients effectively and continuously, offering opportunity routes to waged employment.

Most "continuing care" clients are either unwilling or unable to engage in employment. This partly reflects the current benefits system, which can heavily penalise those seeking work, and partly the lack of local opportunities. Many people are too severely disabled by their psychiatric symptoms or lack confidence and skills required to tackle the ladder to open employment. For those not in employment traditional psychiatric day-care may offer structured activities that provide the latent functions of work (Holloway, 1989), with consequent psychological benefits to the attender. Increasingly emphasis is being put on facilitating the use of mainstream services, such as adult education classes, recreation centres and local community centres. Some people may just want a welcoming place where they can meet other people and have a cheap meal. Others may benefit from a highly structured programme of activities either within a day unit or at a number of different locations. As opportunities for day activities expand in a locality, the need for coordination between units increases; this is an obvious function of the continuing care team.

Although emphasis is rightly placed on the social significance of day care, activities can help users to develop new skills (such as shopping, cooking, budgeting, interpersonal skills) and develop their social networks. Befriending schemes can complement formal day-care by offering a vital opportunity for clients to develop new relationships (Sang, 1989). The day unit can be a place where specific therapies (individual, group, family, behavioural) take place. Some attenders receive much needed personal care whilst others require close monitoring of their mental state (Holloway, 1988). Day-care may, in certain circumstances, provide an acceptable alternative to inpatient admission during periods of psychiatric crisis (Creed, Black and Anthony, 1989).

## Residential services

The majority of people suffering from long-term mental health problems live either alone or with their families. Only a small minority make use of specialist residential services, partly because these services are pitifully inadequate. There are a number of useful literature reviews on residential care for the mentally ill (e.g. Carpenter, 1978; Garety, 1988; Gibbons, 1988). Unfortunately contemporary information on the quality of residential care in Britain is lacking. It is only recently that the rundown of large psychiatric hospitals has been accompanied by careful assessment of residents' needs and the subsequent development of a network of residential provision (NUPRD, 1989). A spectrum of support, from intensively staffed units to supported independent housing within the community, is required to replace the traditional hospital (NUPRD, 1989). Assessment measures are now available to quantify local need within this spectrum (Clifford, 1988; Mullhall, 1989).

Despite a broad consensus over what is required the planning and development of residential provision is often marked by arguments over competing philosophies or ideologies of care. Protagonists may adopt a civil libertarian, anti-institutional stance (Bachrach, 1978), they may emphasise the provision of a rehabilitative environment that facilitates skills development (Watts and Bennett, 1983, 1991; Shepherd, 1984) or they may espouse the tenets of social role valorisation with its concern that the individual be facilitated to adopt valued social roles (Wolfensberger, 1983). Although these differences have considerable value in raising significant issues, it is important that the evolving residential services take account of the nature of severe psychiatric disability, which is not necessarily a product of the institution and the "medical model".

Some hospital patients prove particularly hard to place, often as a result of previous or continuing aggressive, sexually inappropriate or otherwise socially unacceptable behaviour (NUPRD, 1989). Such "challenging behaviours" are hard to define and are certainly context-dependent (see Hogg and Hall, 1992); as a result the epidemiology of the problem is totally obscure. The traditional solution is the large mental hospital, with its locked wards and extensive campus. A small number of "Hospital Hostels", set up to provide an alternative to the traditional mental hospital, have been extensively researched. They have been found to provide an acceptable standard of care within a relatively homely environment and an improved quality of life to residents (Garety and Morris, 1984; Gibbons and Butler, 1987; Simpson, Hyde and Farager, 1989). However, hospital hostels are not a comprehensive alternative since some residents cannot be adequately contained within these settings. Other models include an "asylum community" on a hospital campus (Wing and Furlong, 1986) which could cater for "patients with special needs". Attempts have been made to characterise the potential users of such a campus, who might include people who are elderly, demented and behaviourally disturbed; people with coexisting learning difficulty and major mental illness; people who are brain-damaged and assaultative; those suffering from functional psychoses who are assaultative; and people who are diagnosed as suffering from chronic schizophrenia and present socially unacceptable or self-injurious behaviours (Gudeman and Shore, 1984). At the other philosophical extreme lies the provision of "ordinary housing" for two to four "challenging" residents in intensively staffed houses on ordinary streets. This latter model has been applied with some success to services for people with learning difficulties (Mansell, 1986). There is also an expanding network of private psychiatric hospitals that offer (at a price) treatment and containment for those difficult to place patients who cannot be provided for within their localities.

With the exception of the hospital hostels, evaluations of residential alternatives to hospital care are largely unavailable. A number of studies are now under way. American experience calls into question the role of nursing homes as an alternative to hospital care for elderly people with chronic mental illnesses (Mollica, 1983; Brown, 1985; Talbot, 1988). Clinical outcomes in this context may be closely correlated with expenditure (Linn et al., 1985). Foster-care, landlady and family placement schemes are useful components of a residential care system (Linn, Klett and Caffey, 1982; Anstee, 1985; Howat et al., 1988). The traditional group home seems less relevant to current demand, which is for independent living with the necessary support. Unfortunately the many innovative schemes have been inadequately evaluated. For those with greater needs, emphasis is now on various forms of supported housing within which non-professional workers provide "social care" for residents. The intensity of staffing and professional back-up to these "ordinary housing" schemes varies, as does the organisational context of the scheme (NUPRD, 1989). It is as yet unclear how viable innovative alternatives to the traditional mental hospital that are based on the ordinary housing model will prove to be in the long term. One major difficulty of the ordinary housing model is its high unit costs when compared with traditional services which enjoy some economies of scale. Management of these dispersed services, that are often in the voluntary sector, is also problematical.

The major barrier to the development of residential services is lack of adequate revenue and, even more acutely, capital funding (Mahoney, 1988). Constraints are likely to be exacerbated, at least in the short term, by changes in the financing of "social care", including residential, day and domiciliary services, which is to be channelled through the local authority social service department (HMSO, 1989a). Budgets will not be ring-faced against competing demands on limited local authority resources, and may in any case not reflect the degree of local psychiatric morbidity. Unless services are defended at a local level it is difficult to be optimistic about the immediate future for new forms of residential care in Britain, despite a recent explosion of innovative developments.


### Dealing with crises


Continuing care clients are prone to recurrent crises because of exacerbation in psychiatric symptomatology and breakdown in social supports. Community-based teams that include experienced mental health professionals can be highly effective in preventing hospital admission when an acute crisis occurs (Hoult, 1986). A central issue is whether, when a crisis cannot be contained, use should be made of existing acute psychiatric in-patient facilities or alternative facilities should be developed. Busy acute wards in a DGH unit may provide a highly stressful environment and therefore exacerbate psychotic symptomatology while failing to maintain instrumental skills (see Chapter 2). Acute unit staff, unused to people with continuing disability, are also likely to have difficulty in judging when a patient whose symptoms respond only partially to treatment can appropriately be discharged.

A number of options need to be explored to improve the care of long-term clients who are in acute crisis. The simplest is to improve liaison between the continuous care team and the acute unit. The need for admission may be identified in advance. Clear aims for inpatient care may be identified and the continuing care team may remain involved in management decisions throughout the inpatient episode. Alternatively, separate inpatient services might be provided for patients with long-term disabilities. This would only be practical in districts where psychiatric morbidity is particularly high. The importance of respite services for people with long-term mental health problems, long acknowledged in the care of elderly people suffering from dementia, has not been adequately recognised (Talbott and Glick, 1986). Interestingly a "respite house" has been included in the plans for the replacement of a mental hospital (NUPRD, 1989), although the operation of respite services for the mentally ill has not been adequately evaluated.

## FUTURE DIRECTIONS

Much is now understood about the failings of previous service delivery systems (Martin, 1984b). Unfortunately past failures are often explained in terms of the prevailing ideology; the very real needs of the client group and care staff are often ignored. Although current rhetoric in Britain rightly emphasises the importance of the individualised assessment of the needs of people in receipt of continuing care services (HMSO, 1989a), there are grounds for severe concern about the future. It is possible that the understandable attempts to promote cost-effective services will result in a diminution in the real resources available to provide care for people with long-term mental health problems. Other more politically favoured client groups may gain. The transfer of responsibility for "social care" to local authorities represents a major challenge to health care professionals, who will be required to develop new skills in consultancy with the plethora of providers what will emerge within the "mixed economy of care". The service system in Britain is likely to become more fragmented, at a time when the need for an integrated local mental health authority has at last been recognised in the USA (NIMH, 1987; Lehman, 1989).

Continuing care teams may be allowed to combine the case management function outlined in "Caring for People" (HMSO, 1989a) with direct clinical care. This tenuous possibility, together with increasing involvement in the needs of the long-term mentally ill shown by general practitioners (Kendrick, 1990) and the stirring of a primary consumer movement anxious to ensure good quality services provide the only elements of optimism in an otherwise depressing view of the future. It is all too likely that depleted hospital services will struggle to care for patients in isolation from cash-limited social care services, within which the lack of mental health expertise is not alleviated by awareness of resources within the local community. Clinicians and managers with responsibility for local health, housing and social services need to work together if quality services for people with long-term mental health problems are to emerge from the decaying asylums.

## REFERENCES

Abrams, P. (1977) Community care; some research problems and priorities. *Policy and Politics*, **6**, 125–51.

Anstee, B.H. (1985) An alternative form of community care for mentally ill; supported lodging schemes ... a personal view. *Health Trends*, **17**, 39–40.

Audit Commission (1986) *Making a Reality of Community Care*, HMSO, London.

Bachrach, L.L. (1978) A conceptual approach to deinstitutionalisation. *Hospital and Community Psychiatry*, **29**, 573–8.

Bachrach, L.L. (1988) Defining chronic mental illness: a concept paper. *Hospital and Community Psychiatry*, **39**, 383–8.

Bachrach, L.L. (1989) Case Management; toward a shared definition. *Hospital and Community Psychiatry*, **40**, 883–4.

Barton, R. (1959) *Institutional Neurosis*, John Wright, Bristol.

Bassuk, E.L., Rubin, L. and Lauriat, A. (1984) Is homelessness a mental health problem? *American Journal of Psychiatry*, **141**, 1546–50.

Beard, J.H., Propst, R. and Malamud, T.J. (1982) The Fountain House model of psychiatric rehabilitation. *Psychosocial Rehabilitation Journal*, **5**, 47–53.

Bennett, D. (1983) The historical development of rehabilitation services. In: F.N. Watts and D. Bennett (eds), *The Theory and Practice of Psychiatric Rehabilitation*, John Wiley, Chichester.

Bion, W.R. (1989) *Experiences in Groups*, Routledge, London.

Bluglass, R. (1988) Mentally disordered prisoners; reports but no improvements. *British Medical Journal*, **296**, 1757.

Bockhoven, J.S. (1954) Moral treatment in American psychiatry. *Journal of Nervous and Mental Diseases*, **124**, 167–94 and 292–320.

Borus, J. (1981) Deinstitutionalisation of the chronically mentally ill. *New England Journal of Medicine*, **305**, 339–42.

Braucht, G.N. and Kirby, M.W. (1986) An empirical typology of the chronically mentally ill. *Community Mental Health Journal*, **22**, 3–21.

Brewin, C.A., Wing, J.K., Mangen, S.P., Brugha, T.S., Maccarthy, B. and Lesage, A. (1988) Needs for care among the long-term mentally ill; a report from the Camberwell High Contact Survey. *Psychological Medicine*, **18**, 443–56.

Brown, G.W., Bone, M., Dalison, B. and Wing, J.K. (1966) *Schizophrenia and Social Care*, Oxford University Press, London.

Brown, G.W. and Harris, T. (1978) *Social Origins of Depression*, Tavistock, London.

Brown, P. (1981) The mental health patients' rights movement and mental health institutional change. *International Journal of Health Services*, **11**, 523–40.

Brown, P. (1985) *The Transfer of Care; Psychiatric Deinstitutionalisation and its Aftermath*, Routledge and Kegan Paul, London.

Carpenter, M.D. (1978) Residential placement for the chronic psychiatric patient; a review and evaluation of the literature. *Schizophrenia Bulletin*, **4**, 384–98.

Caton, C., Goldstein, J., Serrano, O. and Bender, R. (1984) The impact of discharge planning on chronic schizophrenic patients. *Hospital and Community Psychiatry*, **35**, 255–62.

Challis, D. and Davis, B. (1986) *Case Management in Community Care*, Gower, Aldershot.

Chamberlain, J. (1988) *On Our Own*, MIND, London.

Clifford, P., Charman, A., Webby, A. and Best, S. (1991) Planning for Community Care: longstay populations of hospitals scheduled for closure. *British Journal of Psychiatry*, **158**, 190–6.

Clifford, P. (1988) *Community Placement Questionnaire*, NUPRD, London.

Clifford, P. and Craig, T. (1988) *Case management systems for the long-term mentally ill. A proposed inter-agency initiative*, NUPRD, London.

Clifford, P., Leiper, R., Lavender, A. and Pilling, S. (1989) *Assuring the Quality of Mental Health Services; The QUARTZ System*, Free Association Books, London.

Coid, J. (1984) How many psychiatric patients in prison? *British Journal of Psychiatry*, **145**, 78–86.

Coid, J. (1988a) Mentally abnormal prisoners on remand; I—Rejected or accepted by the NHS? *British Medical Journal*, **296**, 1779–82.

Coid, J. (1988b) Mentally abnormal prisoners on remand; II—Comparison of services provided by Oxford and Wessex regions. *British Medical Journal*, **296**, 1783–4.

Conway-Nicholls, K. and Elliott, A. (1982) North Camden community psychiatric nursing service. *British Medical Journal*, **285**, 859–61.

Creed, F., Black, D. and Anthony, P. (1989) Day hospital and community treatment for acute psychiatric illness: a critical appraisal. *British Journal of Psychiatry*, **154**, 300–10.

David, A. (1988) On the street in America. *British Medical Journal*, **296**, 1016.

Fagin, L. and Purser, H. (1986) Development of the Waltham Forest Local Mental Health Care Register. *Bulletin of the Royal College of Psychiatrists*, **10**, 303–6.

Falloon, I.R.H. and Liverman, R.P. (1983) Interactions between drug and psychosocial therapy in schizophrenia. *Schizophrenia Bulletin*, **9**, 543–54.

Fenton, F.R., Tessier, L. and Struening, E.L. (1979) A comparative trial of home and hospital psychiatric care: one year follow-up. *Archives of General Psychiatry*, **36**, 1073–9.

Finlay-Jones, R. (1983) The practice of psychiatry in the community. *Australian and New Zealand Journal of Psychiatry*, **17**, 107–8.

Fisher, M., Newton, C. and Sainsbury, E. (1984) *Mental Health Social Work Observed*, Allen and Unwin, London.

Garety, P. and Morris, I. (1984) A new unit for long-stay psychiatric patients; organisation, attitude and quality of care. *Psychological Medicine*, **14**, 183–92.

Garety, P. (1988) Housing. In: A. Lavender and F. Holloway (eds), *Community Care in Practice*, John Wiley, Chichester.

Garety, P. and Toms, R.M. (1990) Collected and neglected: are Oxford hostels for the homeless filling up with disabled psychiatric patients? *British Journal of Psychiatry*, **157**, 269–72.

Georgiades, N.J. and Phillimore L. (1975) The myth of the hero innovator and alternative strategies for organisational change. In: C.C. Kiernan and F.D. Woodford (eds), *Behaviour Modification with the Severely Retarded*, Associated Scientific Publishers, Amsterdam.

Gibbons, J. (1986) *Coordinated Aftercare for Schizophrenia; the Community care information unit*, University Department of Psychiatry, Royal South Hants Hospital, Southampton.

Gibbons, J. (1988) Residential care for mentally ill adults. In: I. Sinclair (ed.), *Residential Care: the Research Reviewed*, HMSO, London.

Gibbons, J.S. and Butler, J.P. (1987) Quality of life for 'new' long-stay psychiatric inpatients: the effects of moving to a hostel. *British Journal of Psychiatry*, **151**, 347–54.

Gibbons, J., Jennings, C. and Wing, J.K. (1984) Psychiatric Care in Eight Register Areas, 1976–1981. *Psychiatric Case Register*, Knowle Hospital, Fareham, Hants.

Goldstein, J.M. and Caton, C.L.M. (1983) The effects of the community environment on chronic psychiatric patients. *Psychological Medicine*, **13**, 193–9.

Grad, J. and Sainsbury, P. (1968) The effects that patients have on their families in a community and a control psychiatric service. *British Journal of Psychiatry*, **114**, 265–78.

Gudeman, J.E. and Shore, F. (1984) Beyond deinstitutionalisation: a new class of facilities for the mentally ill. *New England Journal of Medicine*, **311**, 832–6.

Hawks, D. (1975) Community care; an analysis of assumptions. *British Journal of Psychiatry*, **127**, 276–85.

Henderson, A. (1990) The monitoring of psychiatric patients. *Nursing Standard*, 25 April, 28–31.

Her Majesty's Stationery Office (1975) *Better services for the Mentally Ill*, HMSO, London.

Her Majesty's Stationery Office (1989a) *Caring for People*, HMSO, London.

Her Majesty's Stationery Office (1989b) *Working for Patients*, HMSO, London.

Hoenig, J. and Hamilton, M.W. (1969) *The Desegregation of the Mentally Ill*, Routledge and Kegan Paul, London.

Hogg, L. and Hall, J. (1992) Management of long-term impairments and challenging behaviour. In M. Birchwood and N. Tarrier (eds), *Innovations in the Psychological Management of Schizophrenia*, Wiley, Chichester, pp. 171–204.

Holloway, F. (1988) Day care and community support. In: A. Lavender and F. Holloway (eds), *Community Care in Practice*, John Wiley, Chichester.

Holloway, F. (1989) Psychiatric day care; the users' perspective. *International Journal of Social Psychiatry*, **35**, 252–64.

Holloway, F., Booker, D., Mill, S., Siddle, K. and Wilson, C. (1988) Progress and pitfalls in the move out of hospital. *The Health Service Journal*, 11 August, 910–12.

Hoult, J. (1986) Community care of the acutely mentally ill. *British Journal of Psychiatry*, **149**, 137–44.

Howat, J., Bates, P., Pidgeon, J. and Shepperson, G. (1988) The Development of Residential Accommodation in the Community. In: A. Lavender and F. Holloway (eds), *Community Care in Practice*, John Wiley, Chichester.

Intagliata, J. (1982) Improving quality of care for the chronic mentally disabled: the role of case management. *Schizophrenia Bulletin*, **8**, 655–74.

Jahoda, M. (1981) Work, employment and unemployment; values, theories and approaches in social research. *American Psychologist*, **36**, 184–91.

Johnstone, E.C., Owens, D.G.C., Gold, A., Crow, T.J. and Macmillan, J.F. (1984). Schizophrenia patients discharged from hospital: a follow-up study. *British Journal of Psychiatry*, **145**, 586–90.

Jones, B. (1986) *Treating the Homeless; Urban Psychiatry's Challenge*, American Psychiatric Press, Washington.

Jones, K. and Fowles, A.J. (1984) *Ideas on Institutions*, Routledge and Kegan Paul, London.

Kanter, J. (1989) Clinical case management: definition, principles, components. *Hospital and Community Psychiatry*, **40**, 361–8.

Kay, A. and Legg, C. (1986) *Discharged to the Community*. A review of housing and support in London for people leaving psychiatric care, Housing Research Group, The City University.

Kendrick, T. (1990) The challenge of the long-term mentally ill. *Royal College of Practitioners' Members' Reference Book*, pp. 283–6. Royal College of Practitioners, London.

Kingsley, A., Towell, D. and McAusland, T. (1985) *Up to Scratch: Monitoring to Maintain Standards*, Kings Fund College, London.

Kingsley, S. and Towell, D. (1988) Planning for High-quality Local Services. In: A. Lavender and F. Holloway (eds), *Community Care in Practice*, John Wiley, Chichester.

Knapp, M. (1988) Searching for efficiency in long-term care, deinstitutionalisation and privatisation. *British Journal of Social Work*, **18**, Supp., 151–71.

Kunze, H. (1985) Rehabilitation and institutionalisation in community care in West Germany. *British Journal of Psychiatry*, **147**, 261–4.

Lamb, H.R. (1979) The new asylums in the community. *Archives of General Psychiatry*, **36**, 129–34.

Lamb, H.R. (1984) Deinstitutionalisation and the homeless mentally ill. *Hospital and Community Psychiatry*, **35**, 899–907.

Lamb, H.R. and Goertzel, V. (1971) Discharged mental patients—are they really in the community? *Archives of General Psychiatry*, **24**, 29–34.

Lavender, A. and Holloway, F. (1988) Introduction. In: A. Lavender and F. Hollaway (eds), *Community Care in Practice*, John Wiley, Chichester.

Lehman, A.F. (1983) The well-being of chronic mental patients. *Archives of General Psychiatry*, **40**, 369–73.

Lehman, A.F. (1989) Strategies for improving services for the chronic mentally ill. *Hospital and Community Psychiatry*, **40**, 916–20.

Lehman, A.F., Ward, N. and Linn, L.S. (1982a) Chronic mental patients: the quality of life issue. *American Journal of Psychiatry*, **139**, 1271–6.

Lehman, A.F., Reed, S.K. and Possidente, S.M. (1982b) Priorities for long term care: comments from board and care residents. *Psychiatric Quarterly*, **54**, 181–9.

Lehman, A., Possidente, S. and Hawker, F. (1986) The quality of life of chronic patients in a state hospital and in community residences. *Hospital and Community Psychiatry*, **37**, 901–7.

Linn, M.W., Klett, C.J. and Caffey, E.M. (1982) Relapse of psychiatric patients in foster care. *American Journal of Psychiatry*, **139**, 778–83.

Linn, M., Gurel, L., Williford, W.O., Overall, J., Gurland, B., Laughlin, P. and Barchiesi, A. (1985) Nursing home care as an alternative to psychiatric hospitalization. *Archives of General Psychiatry*, **42**, 544–51.

MacCarthy, B. (1988) The Role of Relatives. In: A. Lavender and F. Holloway (eds), *Community Care in Practice*, John Wiley, Chichester.

Mahoney, J. (1988) Finance and Government Policy. In: A. Lavender and F. Holloway (eds), *Community Care in Practice*, John Wiley, Chichester.

Mangen, S. (1988) Implementing Community Care: an International Assessment. In: A. Lavender and F. Holloway (eds), *Community Care in Practice*, John Wiley, Chichester.

Mansell, J. (1986) *Developing Staffed Housing for People with Mental Handicaps*, Costello, London.

Marlowe, R. (1976) When they closed the doors at Modesto. In: P.I. Ahmed and S. Plog (eds), *State Mental Hospitals: What Happens When They Close?*, Plenum Press, New York.

Martin, F.M. (1984a) *Between the Acts*, Nuffield Provincial Hospitals Trust, London.

Martin, J.P. (1984b) *Hospitals in Trouble*, Blackwell, Oxford.

MIND (1983) *Common Concern*, MIND, London.

Mollica, R.F. (1983) From asylum to community: the threatened disintegration of public psychiatry. *New England Journal of Medicine*, **308**, 367–73.

Muijen, M. (1992) The balance of care. In M. Birchwood and N. Tarrier (eds), *Innovations in the Psychological Management of Schizophrenia*, Wiley, Chichester, pp. 253–76.

Mullhall, D.J. (1989) *Functional Performance Record*, NFER-Nelson, Windsor.

National Institute of Mental Health (1987) *Towards a model plan for a comprehensive community-based mental health system*, Administrative Document. US Department of Health and Human Services.

National Schizophrenia Fellowship (1984) Community care: the sham behind the slogan. *Bulletin of the Royal College of Psychiatrists*, **8**, 112–14.

National Unit for Psychiatric Research and Development (1989) *First Interim Report of the Cane Hill Closure Research Team*, NUPRD, London.

O'Brien, J. and Tyne, A. (1981) *The Principle of Normalisation: a Foundation for Effective Services*, CMH/CMHERA, London.

Patrick, M., Higgit, A., Holloway, F. and Silverman, M. (1989) Changes in an inner city psychiatric in-patient service following bed reduction: a follow-up of the East Lambeth 1986 Survey, *Health Trends*, **21**, 121–3.

Perkins, R.E., King, S.A. and Hollyman, J.A. (1989) Resettlement of old long-stay psychiatric patients: the use of the private sector. *British Journal of Psychiatry*, **155**, 233–8.

Pilling, S. (1988) Work and the Continuing Care Client. In: A. Lavender and F. Holloway (eds), *Community Care in Practice*, John Wiley, Chichester.

Ramon, S. (1988) Community Care in Britain. In: A. Lavender and F. Holloway (eds), *Community Care in Practice*, John Wiley, Chichester.

Renshaw, J. (1988) Care in the Community: individual care planning and case management. *British Journal of Social Work*, **18**, Supp., 79–105.

Richmond Fellowship (1983) *Mental Health and the Community*, Richmond Fellowship Press, London.

Rollin, H.R. (1977) 'Deinstitutionalisation' and the Community: fact and theory. *Psychological Medicine*, **7**, 181–4.

Royal College of Psychiatrists (1980) Community Psychiatric Nursing. A discussion document by a working party of the Social and Community Psychiatry section. *Bulletin of the Royal College of Psychiatrists*, **4**, 114–18.

Royal College of Psychiatrists (1989) Patient advocacy—Report for Public Policy Committee. *Psychiatric Bulletin*, **13**, 715–16.

Sang, B. (1989) The Independent Voice of Advocacy, In: A. Brackx and C. Grimshaw (eds), *Mental Health Care in Crisis*, Pluto, London.

Scannel, T.D. (1989) Community care and the difficult and offender patient. *British Journal of Psychiatry*, **154**, 615–19.

Scull, A.T. (1979) *Museums of Madness*, Penguin, Harmondsworth, Middlesex.

Scull, A. (1984) *Decarceration: Community Treatment and the Deviant*, Polity Press, Cambridge.

Sedgwick, P. (1982) *Psychopolitics*, Pluto Press, London.

Shepherd, G. (1984) *Institutional Care and Rehabilitation*, Longman, London.

Shepherd, G. (1988) The Contribution of psychological interventions to the management of chronic schizophrenia. In: P. McGuffin and P. Bebbington (eds), *Schizophrenia: the Major Issues*, Heinemann, London.

Simpson, C.J., Hyde, C.E. and Farager, E.B. (1989) The chronically mentally ill in community facilities: a study of quality of life. *British Journal of Psychiatry*, **154**, 77–82.

Sinclair, I. (1988) Residential Care for Elderly People. In: I. Sinclair (ed.), *Residential Care: the Research Reviewed*, HMSO, London.

Stein, L.I. and Test, M.A. (1980) Alternative to mental hospital treatment. I. Conceptual model, treatment program and clinical evaluation. *Archives of General Psychiatry*, **37**, 392–7.

Stein, L.I., Diamond, R.J. and Factor, R.M. (1990) A System Approach to the care of Persons with Schizophrenia. In: M.I. Herz, S.J. Keith and J.P. Docherty (eds), *Handbook of Schizophrenia*, Vol. 5, Psychosocial Therapies, Elsevier, Amsterdam.

Stuart, M. (1990) Working Out. *The Mind Guide to Employment Projects*, MIND, London.

Susser, E., Struening, E.L. and Conover, S. (1989) Psychiatric problems in homeless men. *Archives of General Psychiatry*, **46**, 845–50.

Talbott, J.A. (1988) Nursing homes are not the answer. *Hospital and Community Psychiatry*, **39**, 115.

Talbott, J.A. and Glick, I.D. (1986) The inpatient care of the chronically mentally ill. *Schizophrenia Bulletin*, **12**, 129–40.

Taylor, J. and Bhumgara, K. (1989) The Safety Net Project. *Psychiatric Bulletin*, **13**, 677–9.

Taylor, J. and Taylor, D. (1989) *Mental Health in the 1990's: from Custody to Care?* Office of Health Economics, London.

Test, M.A. and Stein, L.I. (1980) Alternative to mental hospital treatment. III. Social costs. *Archives of General Psychiatry*, **37**, 409–12.

Thornicroft, G. and Bebbington, P. (1989) Deinstitutionalisation—from hospital closure to service development. *British Journal of Psychiatry*, **155**, 739–53.

Timms, P.W. (1989) Homelessness and mental illness. *Health Trends*, **21**, 70–1.

Vaughn, C.E. and Leff, J.P. (1976) The influence of family and social factors on the course of psychiatric illness. *British Journal of Psychiatry*, **129**, 125–37.

Wainwright, T., Holloway, F. and Brugha, T. (1988) Day care in an inner city. In: A. Lavender and F. Holloway (eds.), *Community Care in Practice*, John Wiley, Chichester.

Walsh, D. (1985) Case registers for monitoring treatment outcome in chronic functional psychoses. In: T. Helgalson (ed.), *The Long-term Treatment of Functional Psychoses*, Cambridge University Press.

Warr, P. (1984) Job Loss, Unemployment and Psychological well-being. In: V.L. Allen and E. van der Vliert (eds), *Role Transitions*, Plenum Publications, New York.

Watts, F.N. and Bennett, D. (1983) *The Theory and Practice of Psychiatric Rehabilitation*, John Wiley, Chichester.

Watts, F.N. and Bennett, D. (1991) *The Theory and Practice of Psychiatric Rehabilitation*, 2nd edition, John Wiley, Chichester.

Watts, F.N. and Lavender, A. (1984) Rehabilitation Investigation. In: G. Powell and S. Lindsay (eds), *Handbook of Clinical Psychology*, Gower, London.

Weller, M.P.I. (1986) Does the community care? *Public Health*, **100**, 76–83.

Weller, B., Weller, M. and Coter, R. (1987) *Crisis at Christmas 1986*, *Lancet*, **i**, 533–54.

Wing, J.K. (1972) Principles of evaluation. In: J.K. Wing and A.M. Hailey (eds), *Evaluating a Community Psychiatric Service*, Oxford University Press.

Wing, J.K. (1983) Schizophrenia. In: F.N. Watts and D. Bennett (eds), *The Theory and Practice of Psychiatric Rehabilitation*, John Wiley, Chichester.

Wing, J.K. and Hailey, A.M. (1972) *Evaluating a Community Psychiatric Service*, Oxford University Press.

Wing, J.K. and Brown, G.W. (1970) *Institutionalism and Schizophrenia*. Cambridge University Press.

Wing, J.K. and Furlong, R. (1986) A haven for the severely disabled within the context of a comprehensive psychiatric community service. *British Journal of Psychiatry*, **149**, 449–57.

Wolfensberger, W. (1972) *The Principle of Normalization in Human Services*. National Institute of Mental Retardation, Toronto.

Wolfensberger, W. (1983) Social role valorization: a proposed new term for the principle of normalization. *Mental Retardation*, **21**, 234–9.

Wolfensberger, W. and Glen, L. (1973) Programme analysis of Service Systems (PASS); a method for the quantative analysis of human services. *Handbook of the National Institute of Mental Retardation*, Toronto.

Wolfensberger, W. and Thomas, S. (1983) Program analysis of Service Systems' Implementations of Normalization Goals (PASSING). *Normalization Criteria and Rating Manual*, 2nd edn, Canadian Institute of Mental Retardation.

Wooff, K. (1992) Service organisation and planning. In M. Birchwood and N. Tarrier (eds), *Innovations in the Psychological Management of Schizophrenia*, Wiley, Chichester, pp. 277–304.

Wooff, K. and Goldberg, D.P. (1988) Further observations on the practice of community care in Salford: Differences between community psychiatric nurses and mental health social workers. *British Journal of Psychiatry*, **153**, 30–7.

# Index

Note: Page references in *italics* refer to figures; those in **bold** refer to tables

*Index compiled by Annette Musker*